survival Gu

survival Guide for widows
by June Hemer and Ann Stanyer

With contributions by Mary Stott, Andrea Ufland,
Agnes Whitaker, Robert Zara

This may be a little out of date! AB.

© 1986 Age Concern England
Bernard Sunley House
60 Pitcairn Road
Mitcham, Surrey CR4 3LL

ISBN 0–86242–049–0

All rights reserved, no part of this work may
be reproduced in any form by mimeograph or
any other means, without permission in
writing from the Publisher.

Designed by Eugenie Dodd

Typeset by Cyphergrafic

Printed in Great Britain by
Ebenezer Baylis & Son Ltd.,
The Trinity Press, Worcester and London

Cover photograph by Elizabeth Lewis

Contents

Preface

I am so pleased that the National Association for Widows, Cruse and Age Concern have combined to produce this excellent book. For far too long widows have had to rely on assorted pamphlets, friends and out-of-date advice for the answers to some of their problems. We all know that no one can cover all the difficulties we encounter, but I am sure that this book will fill most of our needs. One of the most important reasons for its publication is that it is written by experts in a way that we can all understand. The contributors have not only written from their personal experiences but have also researched their subjects in depth. We should all be grateful to them.

I would suggest that this is a book for every widow to read and keep. I also think that doctors, psychiatrists, psychologists, social workers and funeral directors will find it useful in their work and that libraries should put a copy in their reference sections.

I wish the book well and am confident that the *Survival Guide for Widows* will be of great help to those who need wise advice.

Macleod of Borve
  Baroness
  President, National Association for Widows

About this Book

This book has been written mainly for older widows, members of their families and friends who need information about the emotional and practical aspects of widowhood. Becoming a widow can be the most isolating experience in a woman's life; indeed, it has been described as 'the most common single personal catastrophe'. Because most women marry and tend to live longer than their husbands, they do become widowed at some time in their lives. Some women are widowed several times.

The book is divided into three parts. In *'Learning to be a Widow'*, the first part, there are descriptions of grieving, a process which is not fully recognised or understood by most people. The second part *'Coping with Practical Things'* is a guide to everyday decisions you – the widow – will need to consider. You are encouraged to contact people in the community (including volunteers) whose job it is to give advice; and suggestions are made about books, pamphlets and free leaflets which may be useful.

The case histories woven into the text to show how other widows have dealt with problems may help dispel the inevitable feeling that you are alone.

The final part, *'Getting Advice and Help'*, gives details of useful organisations and publications. The index should help you to find your way around Part Two.

We hope that what we have written will give to widows strength when it is needed, a sense of direction when life seems pointless, reassurance through the uncertainty, and make a contribution towards beginning again; we hope that relatives and friends will also be able to use this book to learn more about what it means to be a widow.

In such a short book we have not been able to cover all aspects of bereavement or of the practical problems which you may experience; we would like to have written more, for example, about the needs of widows from different cultural groups and about the effects of different legislation that applies in Scotland. We would also like to have included the needs of widowers, a smaller group but with many problems in common with widows.

June Hemer
Ann Stanyer

Acknowledgments

Royal Life Insurance Limited offered generous financial sponsorship so that the book could reach a wider audience than would otherwise have been possible.

Although Royal Life stress the need for forward financial planning, they recognise the plight of many elderly people who have been unable to invest in life insurance and other financial provisions.

Margaret Adolphus, of Age Concern, identified the need for this book and brought together writers from two major organisations concerned with the bereaved – Cruse and the National Association of Widows. The authors are indebted to: Virago Press for allowing Mary Stott to write a contribution based on a chapter in her book *Before I Go;* Lee Bennett, of Age Concern who skilfully edited the manuscript; Anne Wilson and staff of the Widows' Advisory Service; and Age Concern who have prepared the manuscript; staff at the Department of Health and Social Security, Department of the Environment and the Inland Revenue for checking drafts; the many widows who have both shared their experiences with us and commented on the drafts.

About the Authors

June Hemer founded the National Association for Widows in 1971, primarily as a pressure group seeking an improved tax position and better pensions for widows. She currently organises the association's national Widows' Advisory Service. She helps individual widows to deal with their problems and represents widows at tribunals.

Ann Stanyer is Principal Lecturer in Social Policy at Coventry (Lanchester) Polytechnic and Honorary Adviser to the Widows' Advisory Trust and has helped individual widows with social security and other problems. She has written widely on welfare rights issues particularly as they affect widows.

Mary Stott is a freelance journalist and a trustee of the Widows' Advisory Service Trust. She is perhaps known best for her editing of *The Guardian* Women's Page and her involvement with the Women's Movement. She has written about her own bereavement in *Forgetting's No Excuse* and more recently about how she has come to terms with being a partnerless woman, again in her books *Ageing for Beginners* and *Before I Go*.

Andrea Ufland is financial adviser to the Widows' Advisory Service and offers women free advice on financial matters. She goes around the country talking to women's groups and organisations and regularly holds money workshops for women. These are attended (and enjoyed) by women of all ages, both rich and poor. She has contributed to workshops and seminars run by the Widows' Advisory Service Trust.

Agnes Whitaker, who died suddenly from cancer in January, 1986, was a freelance journalist and publications editor for Cruse. She specialised in writing about the bereaved; she edited the *Chronicle,* Cruse's monthly newsletter for members, and was production editor of *Bereavement Care,* the journal for all who help the bereaved. Recently she compiled an anthology of prose and poetry for those who grieve, *All in the End is Harvest.*

Robert Zara is a solicitor, practising in Coventry. He has helped individual members of the National Association for Widows with their legal problems, has contributed to workshops and seminars run by the Widows' Advisory Service Trust, and has been the Trust's legal adviser since its inception.

Learning to be a Widow

To read what someone else has experienced may help you – as a widow, as a member of her family or as a friend – to understand something of the process of grieving.

As a widow you may feel that the only person who can truly understand what you are going through, or have gone through, will be another widow. Even close family and friends seem unable to give you the support that you need – not because they do not understand but because they cannot understand. Furthermore, you may find that you fail to understand what they are going through in terms of grieving. If you have a son, he will have lost a father; if you have a niece, she will have lost an uncle. It is not only the widow who grieves the loss of her husband. Often straightforward relationships become strained at times of bereavement when they need to be easy; misunderstandings may arise over stupid little matters; friends may be lost or become distant when they are most needed.

By trying to understand the stresses and strains which are brought about by the death of a loved one, the more likely you are to be able to minimise problems. The first few months of bereavement can bring great swings of temperament, difficulty in sleeping, even physical symptoms of illness; eventually, these pass and you will feel like a whole person again.

Real Tears

It is hard to describe the early reactions to losing a lifelong partner; Margaret Barrow here captures the essence of what she felt at the time.

It's the most odd thing when you're widowed, you're empty. When you see a dead person they seem to be a shell, nothing, finished.

When you're widowed you can walk and talk vaguely, but what an effort. You try to behave normally when so empty, with no brains, no organs. You feel that if someone poked you it would make a hole, so you must not be touched. You watch TV, you see yourself watching; you feel between Heaven and Hell not knowing what you watched. Reading is the hardest; words, letters, vowels, consonants, sentences – all are meaningless. I must concentrate but my mind keeps floating away somewhere, somewhere empty. There's no escape - nowhere to go to get away from being invisible. People talk and I want to look behind to see who they are talking to.

Now I must try; think of one thing at a time; get up; dressing gown. . . that's right. . . ooh slippers. . . zip up before opening the curtains; one thing at a time. Put on the kettle; keep my mind straight – no letting it wander; yes that's right, open the bedroom window. The post's come - oh dear, it's taking all my energy to do things; I can't cope with the post. People say I'm stronger, so I must be. I wonder how the weak ones manage.

I pretend I'm married. I decide to do the things on the same days; yes that would help till time heals. Yes, I'll wash my hair every four or five days; I'll shop once a week – not daily – pretending it's for someone else too. It's church on Sundays – I can do that backwards. I'll join things, filling up the emptiness with things to do - till I'm well. I remember after an illness one should start with milk and water. Perhaps with time, maybe years, it could be cream again? Not yet it isn't. Will it ever be, do you think? Some people have never had cream, so I'm lucky; I've tasted, oh yes, moments of pure cream.

My mind still wanders; there's no anchor. I try to hold on but 'it' keeps slipping away. I talk stupidly: I hear myself and think 'stop it woman'. If I talk a lot I'm holding on; if I stop I get lost somewhere! My children will think 'I didn't know my mother was like that. . . she's nothing'. But I was something once, oh such a long time ago. When the day is over and you've done your best, there's the luxury of crying quietly under the bedclothes – real tears. I must be alive.

How I Learned to be a Widow

Mary Stott describes here how she herself managed to crawl through the tunnel of grief.

Since I learned to be a widow I have always thought that the lucky ones amongst the three million of us in this country are those who felt they had to go on, right from the day following the funeral. Some of us have teenagers who have to be got up, fed and seen off to work or school. Some of us have older children going through the frustration and misery of unemployment or the trauma of marriage break-up. How can we desert them in their hour of need? And some of us have jobs and are conditioned to accept that you always turn up for work unless you are in bed with 'flu or housebound with a broken leg.

In these early days almost all us of are exhausted in every fibre of our being. Grief works like that. Perhaps this exhaustion is Nature's anaesthetic, preventing us from thinking too much about the future, even dulling the intolerable pain of being chopped in half. But anaesthetics wear off. Probably by the time you read these words you have confronted the fact that from now on you are on your own, and have begun to wonder 'What is the point of it all?'.

All 'normal' people accept as a matter of course that it is better to be alive than dead. 'Poor old so-and-so' we say of someone who has died, unless he or she was very old or very ill for a long while. But now you look at life from the outside, as it were. Why is it good to be alive? Why is this sort of half-life you are living now supposed to be more desirable than not existing at all? You look at your home, your job, your garden, your everyday life and you ask yourself 'What's it all for?'. That is why I say that it is a good thing to have to keep going. I know, as everyone knows who has experienced this desolation of the spirit, that the only way to get through is to live each day at a time, thankful when it is over and you can retire to your lonely bed. You have to think of yourself as crawling through an apparently endless dark tunnel. Some day you will see a glimmer of light ahead, I promise you.

Because I wrote about learning to be a widow, not very long after my husband died, and again in my first book, *Forgetting's No Excuse,* widows have written to me over the years, sharing their experience with me. Nearly always they confirmed my own. 'Work is the only answer'; 'We each have our private hell to go through'; 'When my husband died an old friend said 'It will take some time to re-order your life but you will do it because there is so much to do'.

Keep doing

I think that there is the clue to learning to crawl through the tunnel. Keep doing. Of course, one is battling against that persistent fatigue and against a deep-rooted reluctance to take on any responsibilities. But many of us start by doing long-put-off jobs in the home. There is a strange therapy in this. I myself set about clearing all rubbish out of the cellar and then white-washing the walls and painting every door pale blue. A friend who had a similar urge whitewashed all the walls and ceilings of her home, which had become discoloured through her smoking. 'I think', she told me 'it was something to do with wiping out the last five years of my husband's life, when things were so difficult for us'. Later she had everything re-papered and re-curtained in matching material. . . pink peonies, red and yellow roses and blue delphiniums. . . a bit startling to the visitor, but it lifted her spirits. . . as a new white topped dining table and pink and white rose curtains lifted mine.

Nothing would have dragged me away from my home

People who say to the newly bereaved 'You won't want to go on living here, with all those memories' don't, literally, know what they are talking about. They haven't experienced themselves the way the home you and your partner lived in so long can be a strong support. At the time of my bereavement I wrote 'I who knew very well the likelihood that I would one day be a widow but always imagined that if it happened I would run to a very dear friend. In the event, I found nothing would have dragged me away from the home which was the crown of our thirty years of happy life together'. Many years later a widow wrote to me, 'I was desperately lonely. Everyone seemed to leave me alone, because I was a widow, thinking I wouldn't want to be disturbed, I suppose. But I couldn't go. Everything here was associated with my husband and our life together. It would have been like prising me out of the womb. I grumbled about the place but it just wrapped itself around me'. Another widow commented wryly 'It would have been a bleak prospect to move somewhere where there was nothing of him at all'.

Light at the end of the tunnel

I have no doubt that after the loss of the will to live – and perhaps contributing to it – the worst danger for the bereaved is self-pity. 'Why did it have to happen to me?' 'How awful my life is compared with Mrs A, Mr B and Miss C.' If you are ever going to reach that glimmer of light at the end of the tunnel you have to fight self-pity with every scrap of strength you can dredge up. So your husband waved goodbye at the gate when he left for work, and you never saw him alive again? I know a woman who was told, as gently and kindly as possible by her host at a christening party, that her husband had died from a totally unexpected heart attack while on a business trip to Singapore. So your husband went to the lavatory during the night and collapsed on the floor? I knew a woman whose husband was so seriously injured in a car crash that he lay in a coma for a year before he died and never was able to speak to her again. So your husband died of cancer and was in vile pain for months? I know people whose nearest and dearest became senile, and less than human, after years of gradual loss of memory, mind and reasoning faculty. It seems inescapably true that however hard it was for you, it was worse for someone else.

Others suffer too

And we have to remember that it isn't only widows who suffer. There are parents who lose children in accidents or through being hooked on drugs. There are wives whose husbands inexplicably and even without warning walk out on them and set up with some girl young enough to be their daughter, inflicting humiliation as well as grief.

Accepting all this is a reminder that we ought to try to cope. . . but how? Nearly all widows say they are desperately lonely and the assumption is often made that people shun the widow, finding her an embarrassment, with her load of grief; or even, alas, a threat, because she may be 'on the prowl'. (If only people knew how few widows can face even the possibility of a physical relationship with any man, in these early days.) But I think the loneliness mainly comes from within and that after bereavement one somehow seems to lose the knack of 'relating' to other people. There is a sort of creeping paralysis of the social responses. Our ability to be comfortable with other people is more precarious than we realise. It rests on a sort of inner security which may be destroyed by the death of a beloved partner – or by being made redundant, failing in business or in marriage, losing a newborn baby or any other disaster.

At this time we are hyper-sensitive. If a neighbour on the way to the shops hurries past with a wave and no more than a 'Good morning', we tend to think she wants to escape from us. If we are not specifically invited to a coffee morning or office party, we tend to think they assume we shall be a wet blanket. Once upon a time – remember? – we were quite glad to be let off the hook of sociability now and then. It was good to be alone for a little while, to catch up on little odd jobs about the house, to sit and read or sew or knit. Now, being alone means being truly, psychologically lonely, shut in with one's not very likeable, broody, suspicious, self-doubting self.

I think that only a widow who, like me, has managed to survive this period and get involved in life again has the right to say to other widows who are still at the beginning of the tunnel of grief, that the best therapy is to try, as soon as you can, to respond to other people's needs. It sounds so trite, so patronising. But it is true. It is this involvement of 'sisters' that makes the National Association for Widows such a wonderful resource. They know what you know. You know what they know. You can hold out a hand and it will be grasped. You can put an arm around a shoulder and know there will be a grateful response.

It is discovering that one is wanted and needed that begins to melt the wall of ice that has cut us off – we are set on our way towards the light at the end of the tunnel. Out there, there is a new, different and quite interesting life awaiting us. The beloved partner and friend whom we have lost would want us to reach out for it, wouldn't he?

It is more than eighteen years since Mary Stott was widowed and went through the experiences she has shared in this book. Here she writes about her lifestyle and attitudes in later life.*

And so to the future

Because I was widowed a few months before my sixtieth birthday, I can talk more helpfully, I think, to women who have lost a lifetime partner than to younger women whose marriage is tragically severed while their children are still very young. Here I am writing about moving into old age without a 'prop and stay', someone to share both the difficulties and fears of growing old and the genuine pleasures.

---

* *This section is adapted from the chapter 'Growing Old' in her latest book Before I Go.*

Not enough chaps to go round

Social workers always insist that the worst problem of widowhood, especially in later years, is loneliness, and there is a stark, inescapable statistic which we all have to accept. There are three million widows and 800,000 widowers in Britain. Not enough chaps to provide for us all the comfort and joy, ever again, of a dearly-loved man about the house. And the unattached men who might be interested in a late marriage have plenty of choice among young women, and assume that it is some law of nature that a man can always find a mate younger than himself. I think this situaton is changing and will change still more as time goes on, for there are more men than women in younger age groups, and as women are tending to lead more stressful lives and to smoke more and drink more, they may be running more risk, I fear, of early death from lung cancer or heart disease, which at present are more prevalent among men. The balance of the population is changing and is likely to change further.

But for most of us who have been widowed during the last twenty years or so there is precious little hope of a new partnership. We widows always have an inner loneliness which nothing can remove completely. I don't believe there is any substitute for the pair bond, and when death severs it the survivor must always be aware of being 'alone' in a way those who have remained partnerless are not.

But we need not, and indeed should not, go through the rest of our lives pitying ourselves. It is not impossible to find new friends, develop new interests, find reasons of all kinds to go on living. I have, myself.

Things are still there to enjoy

Many of the things you have always enjoyed are still there to enjoy. The coming of spring still lifts your heart – the daffodils under the cedar tree, the grass becoming quintessentially green, the forsythia outside your bedroom window turning to a blaze of gold, the magnolia blooms opening as if they were living mother-of-pearl. If you have no garden, there are other people's trees and flowers. I remember walking down our road a few years ago and finding an old man with a dog standing in a sort of stunned rapture at the beauty of an ornamental pink-blossomed cherry tree.

If music has been your special thing, it may for a while cause painful emotions but in time the enjoyment returns. So far as listening is concerned, we in the last quarter of the 20th century have riches unknown to our forbears, in radio, TV, gramophone records and cassettes. I have been discovering with delight, this last year or two, that

I can record from my 'music centre' on to tapes, even old tapes, music that particularly pleases me, and then play it back whenever I choose. The newer machines, like mine, do not accommodate the old seventy-eight records. Perhaps some enterprising Age Concern or Pensioners' Link or Help the Aged or widows' group might install an older model at one of their centres so that old people could bring their treasured seventy-eight Clara Butt, or Paul Whiteman or Maurice Chevalier, record it on tape, and sit happily of an evening listening to the music of their youth. I still have records of Elizabeth Schumann, Fritz Kreisler, Alfred Cortot, and so forth, now scarcely heard on the air.

Affection from the young

These solitary pleasures do help, but the best help of all in my widowhood and old age has been the readiness of young women friends to give and to show me affection. Customs have changed in recent years, and I am very thankful for it. I know that it is not because I am nicer that I receive more evidence of liking and affection in my seventies than I did in my fifties; it is just that there has been a change in social mores, owing partly to the fact that the women's movement has given women greater feelings of fellowship, sisterhood, comradeliness, call it what you will. (If anyone gets up to give me a seat on the bus or tube, it is likely to be a young woman nowadays.) And partly because the cult of youth has its pleasant as well as its unpleasant side, the young do not feel so in awe of us as we were of our grandparents.

Part of the enjoyment of my autumnal years is a product of my lifestyle since bereavement. Many young friends are deeply involved in the same causes I am involved in, as well as in the same leisure pursuits. I think it heartens them to know that a woman in her seventies still cares about what they care about and is happy to work alongside them, not as a leader but as a 'sister'.

I count my blessings

Sometimes I find myself saying something like, 'If you're lonely, it's your own fault', which must, especially to kind and concerned social workers, make me sound rather like the sort of middle-class suburban Tory living in the prosperous south-east who asks the unemployed why they don't get on their bikes and go and look for a job.

I do count my blessings, of which far the most important is good health. I have had too many friends whose lives have been ruined by arthritis, Parkinson's disease, some degree of paralysis after a stroke, even total incapacity, and one very dear friend whose mind has completely gone – the most awful affliction that could befall any of us, or our families. But there are, thank heaven, a great many more of us elderly widows in tolerably good health, able to get about, look after ourselves and do something for someone else than there are those who become dependent on others for their survival. And one can actually have fun as well as satisfaction in 'doing good' or campaigning, as many a member of the National Association for Widows knows.

One of the most enterprising and enjoyable local ventures I have heard of is TAP – Tooting Action for Pensioners – run by a small group of local people whose outstanding spokeswoman is a widow, vivacious, energetic Olly Hollingsworth. TAP sends representatives to Greater London campaigns for improved pensions and benefits, and also tackles basic local problems like the hazard of broken paving stones by surveying, photographing and reporting on them to the local council. In Wandsworth there is a 'Dial-a-ride' service for pensioners, and not only for necessary visits to the doctor, the clinic or the shopping centre. Their leaflet says: 'Dial-a-ride is not just for necessary trips; use it for fun. Go to the park or the pubs, the shops or the zoo; visit a relative or get involved in local community affairs'.

Sociologists and social workers are also apt to think that they know better than we do what we widows and elderly people really want. 'What they want is choice' they proclaim with generous sympathy and total conviction. 'Choice gives you dignity, and to provide free choice, cash in the pocket is always preferable to hand outs and benefits, however generously administered. The only guarantee of independence, dignity and freedom from patronage or charity is a secure income.' I agree that these sentiments sound admirable, and I have used this line of reasoning myself when arguing that what women need for a happy and successful marriage is economic independence.

Inflation and independence

But in the case of pensions and benefits the argument has a flaw. Pensions may be meant to be secure income; it could even be so if politicians insisted that pensions really kept up with prices. But to people who grew up in a time when inflation was only a word that had something to do with blowing up balloons, it does not 'feel' secure. Inflation presses upon older widows and pensioners not only financially but psychologically, the psychological impact perhaps being the worse of the two evils.

If you grew up before the war, were married and running a household before the war, you remember that a bag of coal cost two shillings (10p) and that you knew how many bags you needed per week. Eggs were a shilling (5p) a dozen. Half-a-crown (12½p) was a substantial sum which would buy you a nice lunch in a good restaurant.

Yes, I know that in those days £400 a year was thought to be a very good salary – less than many people now earn per week. But what the post-war people do not seem able to understand is that our thinking about money is not like theirs. I sometimes feel as if my mental processes in relation to the cost of living have gone on the blink. But there it is. If organisations concerned with the welfare of widows and older people convince the government, any government, that £2 a week on the pension is better than subsidised bus passes I don't think they will be doing us a service.

It is for this reason that I feel we ought to explore the idea of subsidised heating, certainly for older retirement pensioners, and for elderly widows and those in poor health as well. The inclusion in the pension book of a clutch of coupons with which any fuel bill could be paid, in part or in whole, might save many deaths from hypothermia every winter. Gas and electricity bills creep up and up in the offices of British Gas and the electricity boards. Not many elderly persons, like me, have the will or the ability to keep track week by week of how many therms or electricity units we are using. Many old people must dread the quarterly bills and therefore switch off the heat and retire to bed to keep themselves warm. On cold winter days, I often wrap myself in a floor length quilted polyester coat rather than switch on the central heating before evening. It is possible to get a heating allowance, but few of us like doing this, and applications of this kind are not easy – as my experience with my local rating authority suggests.

Being a single householder on a small income, I decided to enquire whether I might be entitled to a rate rebate just after the spring instalment had been paid. Months went by and the autumn demand arrived. After writing to enquire plaintively, 'Do I have to pay or do I not?', a kind and courteous employee of the rating office called, checked over my income and outgoings and took away certain documents which he returned quite promptly. But still no news from the borough treasurer's office until the next spring's rate demand fell due – I then was told that on a rate demand of £426.60 my rebate was £4.29.

Hilariously amused, and resolving never to put myself, or the borough treasurer's department, to the trouble of making or assessing any further application, I wrote to the borough treasurer:

I think perhaps your staff should be congratulated on taking only ten months from the date when I first raised the question of my eligibility for a rate rebate, and thanked for enabling me to settle my account before the next rate demand arrives shortly. I also think the rating authority's generosity should be acknowledged. £4.29 is probably enough to buy a new hot water bottle and a pair of leg-warmers, to help ward off hypothermia.

Needless to say, I had no reply. When, two or three months later, I heard a former chairman of the National Association for Widows tell her story of a rate rebate to the association's annual conference, I wondered if I had not been a trifle too sarcastic. Her munificent rating authority had awarded her a rebate of 48p per half year.

Is it any wonder that some of us feel that free or subsidised transport passes have immediate, positive value, whereas rebates on this and that are hardly worth the worry and the difficulty of applying? Or that we would like to see heating coupons and free telephones for the old and frail?

Life is certainly not easy for us elderly widows, and, in economic terms, it is not likely to get easier in the near future. But let us be thankful if we have good health and are able to keep on our feet; let us remain involved in the community and keep a strong sense of our identity. I am ME as much as I was at 20 or 30. More 'me', in fact, because of all that experience stored in my brain which includes memories of a loving partnership of 30 years which helped to make me what I am.

Old age isn't calm

My mother lived only to see one granddaughter. She never heard a grandchild say, 'I love you Granny; take care'. She missed the very interesting and rewarding years a woman can have in her sixties and seventies. I am sure young women would have shown her as much affection as they have shown me. I wish she'd had what I have. I wish all men and women of my age had as good health and as many friends as I have. Though you have to work for friends, luck also plays a big part in the possibility of keeping them. I saw a poster in a women's centre in London, showing a very old woman and her thoughts. 'Old age isn't calm', she was thinking.

> *Fires burn in the bodies of old women*
> *Flutes sing in their ears and*
> *they fall in love now and then.*

That's right.

It Only Happens to Other People

Agnes Whitaker draws on the experiences of widows to describe the effects of, and reactions to, the loss of a husband.

It only happens to other people. Their husbands die. Somehow you never imagined it would happen to you. But it has happened, either with shocking and unbelievable suddenness, or with a bit of warning, or after a long illness, which may have included periods of buoyancy and hope, which were in the end to prove cruelly false.

There is a strange eerie sense of unreality in the first few days after the death, even if your husband was ill for a long time, and you knew he had no chance of recovery. Proust wrote 'People do not die for us immediately. . . it is as though they were travelling abroad'. Some of you may not believe the death has actually occurred, and yet all the relentless arrangements tell you it did happen. The funeral, letters, cards from relatives and friends, the financial and legal details: all these reinforce the reality of your loss.

Many of you have learned over the years to be very well organised and adaptable, juggling different problems and soldiering on through life with courage and patience. You will probably try to do that now. Above all, it may seem essential to keep control, to take over 'his' tasks as well as yours, to keep a regular routine, to put on a brave front. But as the weeks pass, very few women actually find this possible. The loss is too massive, and enters almost every aspect of your life.

You have lost your closest companion, the person you aired family and other problems with, discussed TV programmes and world issues with, the one with whom you tried out plans and schemes. You have lost someone to cook for, sit beside, go visiting with and welcome guests with. You always took for granted that you would be protected and helped on journeys, and at social events. You have lost the person who was, most probably, your one solace at times of great anxiety, and possibly the person to whom you could admit embarrassing thoughts, or fears of various kinds. You have lost the one with whom you used to share warmth and comfort and closeness. Many of you were 'still sweethearts' in a physical sense.

Some women are used to paying all the bills as well as budgeting. But in many marriages the husband dealt with the tax, the mortgage, insurance, car and house repairs; he repaired the leaking gutter, got the lawnmower going, changed the fuse, put up shelves, made the patio and creosoted the fence. You have probably lost a helpmate in many areas of life.

A massive loss

So it is a massive loss that you have suffered. It is not surprising if you feel very helpless as well as deeply sad. It is no wonder if you cannot keep calm, keep control, keep organised, keep your routine. To expect that is more than any human can manage.

'My husband died of cancer. He fought so hard to live, and I felt so guilty to be alive.'

You may find yourself numbed into an inability to think about the details of the funeral, to think about how to make it personal and memorable, to think of decisions about newspaper announcements, flowers, burial or cremation, or perhaps some sort of family meal. If you have brothers, sisters or children coming to your assistance they can sometimes be most sensitive, making all the preliminary arrangements for you and encouraging you to make the final decisions, so that later on you will feel that you have had some say in the putting to rest of your husband's body.

But sometimes family members may take many of the arrangements out of your hands. This is rarely done from selfish or bossy motives, more usually to spare you what they know to be painful details. It may mean that some special and perhaps symbolic ideas that you would have liked included in the funeral have been omitted. If that does happen bear in mind that it is very difficult for anyone to manage those first few days. Sometimes these omissions can be remedied at a later date; the red roses that were never ordered could be put on the grave to mark your wedding anniversary or you could order a red bush for the crematorium or for your own garden.

There are not always family supporters to hand when an older woman is widowed. You may not have had any children, or they may live abroad. Your brothers and sisters may also live abroad or have died. The sense of isolation can be immediate and frightening. But for everybody there will be someone who will respond in the first days and weeks, so long as you make your needs known. Many funeral directors are especially caring to those who have no family support. Many widows avoid asking for help from their priest or rabbi because they have never been to his church or synagogue, or only rarely in the past. You might be surprised how understanding a clergyman can be if you approach him. Very few will simply preach the gospel at you, and many have a profound understanding of bereavement. Many churches and synagogues have their own lay support groups for bereaved people and one of these could prove to be a lifeline for you.

If you are from another culture

If your background is Muslim, Buddhist, Sikh or West Indian, you may feel an especially strong yearning to be back in your home country at a time when your own rituals are very important. You may find British facilities are unsatisfactory; perhaps they do not give you the helpful feeling that things are being done in the time-honoured way. But many funeral directors and crematorium staff will do their best to adapt their normal arrangements if you explain your particular needs. On the whole they are not uncaring, but some may be unsure with foreigners, and unaware of the significance of certain rituals to you.

One day, hopefully, there will be community interpreters available to all of you who have a language communication problem. This can be very trying when important arrangements have to be made. In the meantime, it is better to have a friend who speaks good English to accompany you when you make these arrangements, so that misunderstandings are avoided. A son or a daughter may not be the most valuable person on such an occasion; his or her grief may make clear and quick thinking difficult.

The pictures we see on television of funerals in the Middle East may be intrusive at moments of personal devastation, but they do also show how other nationalities are able to express outwardly the overwhelming feelings of loss that a close bereavement brings. Perhaps with our Western 'stiff upper lip' attitude, we have moved away from our most natural, most human instincts. In the world's oldest stories handed down to us, there is tearful mourning, and King Lear cries out about his daughter 'Howl! Howl!'. In a way the tears are also a celebration of the depth of his partnership, and a form of remembrance. Seen in that positive sense, perhaps they do not seem shaming any more.

Grief needs an outlet

You may be worried and frightened because you cannot prevent tears coming, and you cannot stop them going on and on. They can start in the most unfortunate places, like the supermarket. You wonder if you have lost all control over yourself. Doctors and nurses will testify how often widowed people weep in their surgeries and clinics. At home the tears can go on and on until you are quite drained and exhausted. Sometimes you will know yourself to be primarily crying out to your lost husband, sometimes crying more in despair at your own helplessness and loneliness. But there is a natural time limit to tearful grieving. Very gradually, sometimes with steps backwards, you will find that breaking down in public is less of a hazard, less likely to happen at home at the smallest recollection, less likely to wear you out by going on and on. For years, however, sudden tears may remain a possibility when very tender memories or associations surface. The rest of a lifetime may not be long enough to accept and understand every aspect of the loss, which is what has to happen before such memories will cease to wound.

An elderly woman found that the most painful feeling in the early weeks of her bereavement was one of shame that she had 'broken down' in tears at the graveside. She and her husband had promised each other to be brave during his long illness, and it had seemed a duty to him to continue this after his death, and especially after the funeral.

Some of you may have the very opposite problem and may find yourself unable to cry. It may be that you have always been used to controlling your emotions, both at home and at work. Perhaps your conscious or unconscious thinking is that if you can control tears then you can control your feelings of grief.

Many widows say they did not cry at all in the first week or two, especially after a sudden death. There is often a sense of numbness, of being in a half-dream, of doing things like an automaton, of not feeling anything very strongly. This can be a natural reaction for a week or two, but if it persists for very much longer than that, then it may be helpful to find someone to share your feelings with. Grief does not go away if you do not allow it an outlet; it just stays buried more deeply within you. You do have to grieve, and grieving is likely to involve some weeping.

You might find that you are comparing your reactions and progress with those of a sister or close friend whose husband died a year before yours. Try not to do this. Every widow has her own way of grieving, her own time span, and it is not necessarily better or worse than another's. The way it goes will be related to your own circumstances and your own personality.

I'm so afraid

Fear, almost panic, that one is also carrying the seeds of some mortal disease seems to be quite common in early bereavement, especially after a sudden death. It can loom up in the small hours of the night. Your heart seems to be palpitating, and you dread that your recent mild digestive or bowel upsets are the beginnings of cancer, for instance.

Because your husband's body so suddenly failed him, you had to face, with no preparation at all, all the trauma of that sudden mortality. At the beginning of that day he had no more life. This fact has shaken you to the roots of your system, shaken your confidence and security in the way things happen, and you probably have not fully acclimatized yet. You therefore feel very vulnerable. Most doctors understand this phenomenon very well, so do go and see your GP, who is likely to be able to reassure you that there is nothing seriously wrong with you.

A woman's husband died in a few minutes after a sudden heart attack. Previously he had seemed a thoroughly healthy man. A couple of months after his death, she began to develop constant fears that she, too, had some severe bodily defect, and would shortly also die.

The other dread that frequently besets those who are grieving is the dread of going mad. The emotions seem so powerful, your own control so poor. You had no idea you could howl and even scream like this.

You are not going mad, and these distressing reactions will not go on for ever. They may be with you every day for a while, but soon you will notice that you had a few quiet hours, and then a whole day passes without that internal heaving, sighing and sobbing. Take note of these quieter days – gradually there will be more and more of them. You are beginning to recover.

Physical symptoms

There are some real bodily reactions to close bereavement – more proof that our bodies and our minds do not work entirely separately. The symptoms can be troublesome, but are not usually dangerous. Perhaps the most difficult is insomnia (sleeplessness), because, without a good night's sleep, we are badly placed to face the challenges, problems and sadnesses of the next day. A decade ago many women were prescribed tranquillisers in such circumstances. Some of them found it hard, even impossible, to wean themselves off the tablets later. Nowadays both doctors and patients are wary of starting down that road, but there are situations when a short course of tablets could be advisable, such as to break the cycle of insomnia, or when it becomes so bad that your body has become quite exhausted. On the whole, however, most women evolve their own pattern of combatting this sleeplessness, until it gradually disappears. Some refuse to take a sleeping pill two nights running, some have an afternoon doze, some have a hot bath and Horlicks at night, some try a natural herbal remedy, or read in bed.

Other bodily ailments which commonly emerge in early bereavement are rashes, backache and menstrual, digestive or bowel disturbances. By all means ask the doctor's advice about them, even if it is just to be reassured that nothing serious is amiss.

Fear is a most destructive emotion. Inside us it eats away at our confidence, our courage and our positive thoughts. We cannot live with any internal peace when we are fearful. We must try to resolve the things that are producing that fear, either with more knowledge and understanding of our own grieving process, or by asking for more support from a friend or counsellor, or by getting the professional opinion of our doctor.

Relief

Mental deterioration of any kind is particularly hard to bear, and the relief a widow may feel is absolutely understandable, and there should be no guilt about it.

In a group discussion a widowed woman voiced her feelings of guilt about the strong sense of relief she experienced when her husband eventually died after slowly going downhill with senile dementia. In the last couple of years he had completely lost his earlier admirable character, and had become inconsistent, selfish, and thoroughly trying to everyone around him. She had borne the brunt of his behaviour.

In a way the husband that this woman knew and loved had been dead for some time. The man who died recently was only the shell of her husband. In the first few weeks after a death following a long period of dementia, the trials of the last months or years will be uppermost in your mind, perhaps causing considerable emotional pain. Gradually the delights and joys of earlier years will be recalled, and the respected man that you loved will re-emerge more strongly in your memory and your heart.

There may be quite a different feeling of relief if there was little love or affection within the marriage in recent years. Some couples stay together for security and stability rather than out of love. Some come to the point where they are frequently maddened by many of their spouse's gestures and remarks – endlessly twiddling the knobs of the radio, and constant criticism of your generosity to the children. So initially the death might be perceived as something of a relief.

Unfinished things

When the marriage has been deeply unhappy or turbulent, with serious issues unresolved, you might imagine that you would not grieve so much, or so long. In fact the reverse is true – it can last longer, and you may have a harder time than those who had a happy marriage. Some of you will have to come to terms with the unfinished things – the healing gestures that could have been made, the very unkind things that still hurt, the anger and resentment over lost opportunities. You may find it helpful to look back to the early days, when there was some promise and satisfaction in your marriage, before communication broke down, or the bitter hurts came which you could not forgive or forget, or your own mistakes, which you regret deeply, and cannot now amend.

It does not help your recovery to pretend to yourself, or to anyone who is supporting you, that the marriage was 'all right really' if it clearly was anything but. Only by accepting the realities of your married life can you find peace and a way forward.

'I was surprised at the intensity of my rage, even though our marriage had been so desperately unhappy.'

How should you grieve for a bad marriage? It is not easily done alone. Indeed much grieving is done by finding another person who will allow you to ventilate all your thoughts, and just listen to you. The problem with this particular subject of marital unhappiness is that you may not want to tell close relatives or friends about it – you would rather remain a closed book for ever.

This is a situation where a bereavement counsellor or another widow really can be a great help. You can voice your anger and bitterness to him or her in complete confidence, knowing that family and friends will never hear of it. Once this is off your chest, you should feel relieved of a big emotional burden, and find that there does not seem to be such a dead end in your grieving. You can begin to see meanings, and pointers to a new life.

Anger

You may be surprised at your fury about some aspect of your husband's death which you feel could have been organised more effectively or sensitively. This anger is therefore often forcibly directed against the doctor or the hospital, the funeral director, the clergyman or rabbi. Sometimes it will be anger against God for allowing the death to happen, sometimes (if you are being honest) with your husband for abandoning you.

Many widows also find they feel anger against themselves, and this is expressed as remorse or self-reproach. You may be deeply regretting that you did not stay at the hospital that extra half-hour, or make some particular arrangement for the funeral. In fact, any alternative decision you might have taken is unlikely to have made any dramatic difference to your husband's welfare, nor to your close relationship together, probably built up over many years. It is our own feelings which are chiefly hurt by these might-have-beens.

'We'd just washed him and changed the bed; I'd gone downstairs to show the district nurse out. When I got back he'd died. It was as though he had not wanted us to see him go.'

Neither anger nor self-reproach of this kind are quite what they seem. In grief we often vent our total helplessness and inability to control the whole situation on to some particular aspect of it. It is commonly the whole fact of the death we are not yet quite accepting when we protest violently in this way. As Dr. Murray Parkes writes in his book *Bereavement:* 'A major bereavement shakes confidence in our sense of security. The tendency to go over events leading up to the loss and to find someone to blame even if it means accepting the blame oneself is a less disturbing alternative than accepting that life is uncertain. If we can find someone to blame or an explanation that will enable the death to be evaded, we have a chance of controlling things'.

Depression

The process of grieving can have some unkind twists to it. One which some of you will meet is the onset of depression. Those of you now in your seventies and eighties may not have heard about depression in your youth, but you will remember relations and friends who had a mild or severe patch of gloom or apathy at some stage. Life seemed purposeless; they sat for hours doing nothing, or toying with something, and none of you could stir them into enthusiasm for anything much. It is hard that depression comes quite commonly to bereaved people just when their worst pangs of grief are starting to subside, and they might be beginning to recover some energy and purpose in life.

Apart from apathy, this depression can show itself as feelings of hopelessness and purposelessness. You can find yourself not as sad as you were, but more gloomy, in low spirits. What is the point of making the house look pretty and welcoming when there is no one to do it for? There is yourself now, and those that visit you from time to time, but your own pleasure and satisfaction seem a very poor reason for making much effort just at the moment. What is the point in sowing seeds, and pricking out plants, and pruning, when you cannot enjoy the results together? If you used to garden together, each season of the year will only emphasise the huge gap in your life.

It is often sensitive, caring people who are prone to depression at hard times – those who notice beauty in small things, and are often profoundly moved by the power of great music. They feel very deeply the poignant details of their situation.

If you accept that you have such low feelings of yourself, and that they are not in the people or circumstances around you, and if you can trust that this is another phase, a patch of the grieving process, then you will be helping yourself towards beginning again. Ahead of you there can be renewed or new confidence, even enthusiasm. Whatever your age in years, and so long as ill-health is not wearing you down, there can be something of a good life in widowhood. At the time of bereavement many widows have 20 to 25 years to live – a third of their lifetime. Although most will later admit that their husband's death was the hardest thing they ever faced, they will show in their lives, in their attitudes and activities that they have found ways of managing, and ways of enjoying life very fully.

Going astray

In marriage a husband can be the most watchful critic as well as the very best of friends. There is probably no one to fulfil that role now, in a loving positive way. So you have to watch yourself for signs of what the Irish call 'giddiness', a tendency to escape from realities.

Promiscuity can be a likely one, especially in younger widows. There is less opportunity when you are past retiring age, though the wish may still be there for some. The commonest is probably the bottle of alcohol. It is the easiest thing to let one or two drinks increase to four or more, and that will wreak havoc with your weekly budget, and provide no permanent solution to your problems. If you feel you are already along this road, do seek help. Tell your doctor for a start.

A newly widowed woman in her sixties dared not tell her children what was happening. In the end she 'phoned a widows' organisation. 'We only ever drank alcohol at Christmas', she said, 'but I tried a couple of sherries one day, and found they did help me forget myself for a while. They've become a daily thing now, and I have to have four or five to get the same effect. I am so worried, and ashamed of what Bill would have thought of me'.

Loneliness

As months go on you may find that the prevailing feeling becomes one of loneliness. This is an immensely common problem with almost every age group and every type of person. For the first time in your life loneliness may hit you sharply and it can remain as a severe residual problem even when you feel you are recovered from grieving. When you are suffering greatly in the early weeks, you may not have the strength or will-power to try to combat the loneliness, but as you notice yourself recovering this is something that you can begin to understand and work on.

Whatever your age or state of health, some progress should be possible, and provided you are adaptable and persistent you may be able to keep the loneliness at bay for much of the time. How do you set about doing this?

Loneliness is a subjective thing. Different people will have very dissimilar feelings about a similar situation. So the most logical way to begin to combat loneliness may be to concentrate on yourself, rather than trying to solve particular situations of loneliness in your life. By accepting the fact that you have no husband to understand, to comfort, to be tolerant, you could start to be more kindly, gentle and understanding with yourself and your own weaknesses, and not expect quite such high standards from yourself. It is mainly a matter of cherishing yourself. You will be able to see the progress that you have made in all sorts of directions, and be pleased with yourself for having achieved it. Buying new towels or chair covers could be one such; you have no-one to buy them for, but you bought them for yourself, for your own satisfaction, to cheer you up. Some widows write down their own accounts of progress, especially in combatting loneliness, either for their own benefit, or to spur others in a group of bereaved folk.

Looking forward to years and years of living in an empty house would be impossibly daunting if you were certain that it would always be as hard as it is at the beginning. But in this instance you can take comfort from the example of other widows; thousands who at first could hardly bear to stay at home, with the emptiness and the silence, have gradually become accustomed to it. Some sort of crutch will be helpful in the early weeks. The voice on the radio helps in the daytime, the TV in the evening, and a book by the bedside. And of course a cat or dog provides some life and response and warm comfort at home.

Searching

One of the most important things we do when we grieve is to go on searching, in various ways, for the person who has died. Even though the rational part of us knows he has gone, another part of us cannot help searching for him, with the intense pangs of grief that make us suffer greatly. Sometimes you may be sure that you saw his familiar profile in a crowded street, and on another occasion you swear you saw him down the garden path. That near-hallucination is nothing to be alarmed at; it is a common phenomenon amongst widowed people. Many of you may also have vivid dreams about your husband at night – perhaps nearly every night for several weeks. The morning wakening is the hardest thing to bear.

In the searching process you find yourself wrestling with some of the deepest and hardest questions men and women have faced in every generation, about the nature and existence of God or providence, and about whether there is any sort of life after bodily death. Some of you may earnestly read poetry, or sacred and religious books, perhaps for the first time in your life, looking for answers. At the present time C.S. Lewis's *A Grief Observed,* Gibran's *The Prophet* and Joyce Grenfell's writings are popular with newly widowed people.

Just like all those generations before us, we will not find any proven answers, because even our insatiable scientists have not found a foolproof way to prove or disprove the existence of God, or a way to find out the nature of life after death, if there be such. But in thinking, and reading, and talking (and some will be praying also) you should eventually find some meaning in the death you are grieving, and meaning in the new single life which you are now living.

Beginning again

It is not possible to recover properly from a close bereavement without grieving. Some of you may not need to grieve very much because you have, up to a point, already accepted the death some time ago – perhaps if your man was much older, or ill for a long time. For the rest of you there is no way round it, either by distracting yourself with busy things, or by forbidding yourself to think about the deepest hurts.

Mercifully, there are some seeds of beginning again in the midst of the hardest, most painful grieving, and you need to watch out for them, take note of them, hang on to them. You will find these seeds in the smallest glimmers of hope during your blackest hours. You might notice that you can laugh in the midst of your tears, that you can begin to forgive old hurts, you can now make more meaningful contact with a friend or daughter or son. These insights may be momentary and difficult to define, but they are strong signs that you are beginning to make a recovery. They are also telling you, in an indirect way, that you will not be overwhelmed or defeated by your loss and grieving, that you have untapped resources within. One day you will be aware that the husband you have lost, far from being lost forever, has become somehow incorporated within you and become part of your being and your life. In this sense love really is stronger than death.

Coping with Practical Things

D uring the first few days of bereavement you can get advice on arranging the funeral and obtaining the necessary documents from your funeral director, doctor or your minister. The DHSS leaflet *What to do After a Death* is also very helpful. This section of the book looks at the most common practical problems which you are likely to encounter as a widow after the funeral; it is a guide to options open to you for dealing with them.

After the funeral one of the first practicalities you have to cope with is your husband's will; the chapter *'Where There's a Will and Where There Isn't'* outlines the various situations which can occur in the process of settling an estate. You may worry about your financial situation; in *'Money to Live On'* the role of State benefits is described. Another fear may be whether you can afford to keep your home; the options which may be available, whether you rent or own your home, are explored in *'Keeping and Maintaining Your Home'*.

The chapter *'Paying the Right Amount of Tax'* will ease any apprehension you may feel about dealing with the income tax authorities. Alternative ways of keeping down costs, paying your bills and, for those fortunate enough to have some capital, making investment plans are explored in *'Making the Most of Your Money'*.

If you feel that you have been subjected to 'bad administration' or have been treated wrongly by a government department, *'Appealing for Your Rights'* will help you to decide whether and how to complain or appeal.

Finally, in *'Making the Most of Yourself'*, June Hemer mentions some of the things that have contributed to the pleasures of her life as a widow – and she also makes some pertinent comments about the proper use of medicines, alcohol and tobacco.

Where There's a Will and Where There Isn't

Robert Zara discusses the situations that can occur when settling your husband's estate.

In Victorian novels, the family solicitor would read the will to the family gathered together for the purpose. This situation is no longer very common, but it is just as important to find and read your husband's will as soon as possible because it may contain instructions about the funeral arrangements. For example, he may have wanted to be buried in a particular plot or may have specified cremation. He may have requested that his body be used for medical research or that parts of his body be used for transplant operations.

Any such wishes are not legally binding, however, and your husband's body may not be used for medical purposes if he has expressed an objection before death (whether in his will or in some other way) or if you object after his death.

If you do not know where your husband kept his will, you should ask his solicitor and the bank. Even if the solicitor does not have the original will, he may have a copy and this may give you the information you need.

If your husband left a will

If your husband has left a will, it should be much easier to settle his affairs. However, wills that have not been properly prepared can cause more difficulties than having no will at all. A properly drawn will normally names one or two people to act as 'executors' – and you may be one of these. The main legal duty of an executor, after making the funeral arrangements, is to administer the estate. This means that the executors must gather together your husband's assets, pay his debts and taxes and distribute what is left in accordance with his will.

It is usual, though not always essential, for executors to apply for a grant of 'probate', which is official confirmation of the executor's right to administer the estate. Probate is usually necessary because some assets will only be handed over to the executors on production of a grant of probate. However, where the sum involved is less than £5,000, probate will not usually be needed. This is so if the money consists of wages and pensions due to servicemen, civil servants and local authority employees. It is also true of money invested in a building society, the National Savings Bank or the Trustee Savings Bank. It does not matter if the total estate is more than £5,000 so long as there is less than £5,000 invested in any particular bank or building society.

Obtaining probate is relatively simple unless the estate is so large that there is a possibility of Capital Transfer Tax* being payable – in which case you should employ a solicitor. Most large towns have an office known as the Probate Registry, and you will find that the officials there will give you all the help you need.

Many people are surprised by the time it can take to 'wind up an estate', particularly if the executors have to account to the Inland Revenue for Capital Transfer Tax. Valuing assets, particularly if they consist of shares in a private company, can take time and may involve negotiations with the Inland Revenue. Currently no tax is usually payable where the total estate is worth less than £71,000. You can get more information on this from your local tax office or the Inland Revenue leaflet *Income Tax and Widows*.

If the estate is taking a long time to administer, it should be possible to pay out some of the money to those due to benefit under the will before the estate is finally wound up. If a solicitor is administering the estate, you should not hesitate to ask him to do this. He should be able to estimate the tax that will be payable with reasonable accuracy.

Contesting a will

It will obviously take longer to settle an estate if the will is contested. A will may be contested even though probate has already been granted. The main grounds for contesting a will are that it was not properly executed (for example, if the will was not witnessed in accordance with the rules), that the 'testator' (the person signing the will) was not of sound mind, or that it was obtained by undue influence or by fraud. Although it is very rare for a will to be contested, if it happens to you, get legal advice from a solicitor.

---

* The March 1986 budget announced the replacement of Capital Transfer Tax by an Inheritance Tax. As the details of the new tax are very complicated, you should ask at your local tax office or write to the Inland Revenue Enquiry Office, Somerset House, Strand, London WC2R 1LB.

Mrs Singh was having difficulty in maintaining her home following the death of her husband. In his will, which had been prepared with the advice of a bank which was also named as the executor, her husband left her a small legacy and allowed her to continue living in the house as long as she wished, provided that she maintained it. (On her death the house would pass to her husband's children by a previous marriage.)

Unfortunately the bank refused to help with the maintenance problems; and when Mrs Singh asked the Widows' Advisory Service what she could do, she was told that the bank was correctly applying the provisions of her husband's will. If she had asked for advice earlier, she could have applied to the Court for more generous provisions from her husband's estate.

Mrs Singh's case shows that even where there is a will, problems can still arise. You should seek advice as soon as possible if you are in any way unhappy about your financial position and the financial provisions in the will.

If your husband did not leave a will

If your husband has died without leaving a will (usually called 'dying intestate'), there are rules to decide who should administer his estate and how it should be distributed.

As his widow, you have the first claim to administer your husband's estate. To do so formally, you will need to apply for Letters of Administration, which have the same effect as a grant of probate. But you do not need to do this in circumstances where it would not be necessary to apply for probate. So, for example, if your husband has left no houses or land but has savings of £2,000 in the bank, you should not need to apply for Letters of Administration. The bank will pay you out the money if you show them the death certificate and sign a simple form confirming that you are entitled to the money.

The rules which govern how your husband's estate will be distributed are rather complicated, and only a summary can be given here. How much you will inherit depends on two things: the size of the estate and the claims of other relatives. There are two situations where you will inherit the whole estate. The first is where your husband has no children or other close relatives who survive him. No matter how large his estate may be, you will be entitled to all of it (after tax). The second situation is where your husband's estate is less than £40,000. Nobody else will have a claim.

You will also inherit your husband's 'personal chattels' – however much they may be worth. These include, for example, cars, domestic furniture, pictures, ornaments, jewellery, musical instruments, wine and consumable stores (if they were not used for business purposes).

If your husband leaves children or grandchildren (the children may be illegitimate) and his estate is worth more than £40,000, the distribution will be different. You will get the personal chattels, the first £40,000 (after tax) of the rest of the estate, and a life interest in half of what is left.

If your husband leaves neither children nor grandchildren but does leave other close relatives, you will get the personal chattels, and up to £85,000 (after tax) from what is left of the estate. If there is anything else remaining, you will get half of it. The figures of £40,000 and £85,000 are varied from time to time by Government order – so you should check with your tax office or solicitor.

Your share of the estate takes priority over the claims of other relatives, even children. Of course, in most cases there will not be enough money in the estate to pay even your share in full and therefore the children or grandchildren or other relatives will get nothing. Their claim is only on what is left after you have been given the capital sum and the personal chattels.

If you wish, you may take your matrimonial home as all or part of your share of the estate. To do this you must have had your home there at the date of your husband's death. You have twelve months from the date of death to exercise this option. In that time the administrators cannot sell the house without your written consent except by order of the Court or to meet debts of the estate which cannot otherwise be satisfied. This right only applies where your husband owned the house. If you owned it jointly, then the house will become yours automatically, as his share in it will be extinguished by his death. If your husband was a tenant protected by the Rent Act, then his tenancy (which cannot be sold) passes to you as long as you continue to live in the house.

When a creditor administers the estate

Mrs Cornford's case, outlined below, illustrates what can happen when a man fails to make a will. It also shows the danger of allowing a creditor (such as a bank) to administer an estate. Mrs Cornford commented in one of her letters to the Widows' Advisory Service that the bank had so far taken about £3,000 for fees and she would have been much better advised to have taken out Letters of Administration herself — as she was entitled to do.

Mr and Mrs Cornford had four children and had been running a farm and a butcher's shop when he died suddenly without leaving a will. Mrs Cornford became entitled to the first £40,000 of her husband's estate. The rest of his estate was to be divided into two halves, one half being payable to the children and the other half being invested for Mrs Cornford during her lifetime. The three eldest children were over eighteen and agreed that they would not take their share; the share of the youngest child, who was under eighteen, had to be put in trust. Subsequently, one of the three older sons changed his mind and decided he did want his share but agreed to wait until his mother died.

Unfortunately Mr Cornford had died leaving a large overdraft and to clear this Mrs Cornford had to sell the butcher's shop. She allowed her husband's bank to take out Letters of Administration to his estate; and after a while the bank told her that it intended to sell the farm to enable Mrs Cornford to receive her £40,000 and the two children to receive their shares.

Mrs Cornford was most distressed by this proposal and she consulted the Widows' Advisory Service. She was successful in persuading the bank not to sell the farm.

If you were separated or divorced

If you were separated when your husband died, you are still legally his widow. Everything written above applies to you unless you were separated by a decree of judicial separation, in which case you will not automatically have a right to inherit anything from his estate if your husband did not leave a will. By law the administrators must distribute your husband's estate on the assumption that you had died before him.

If you are divorced, then of course the death of your former husband does not make you a widow. If your husband made a will in your favour or appointed you as his executor before your divorce, the gift to you will be of no effect nor will your appointment as executor be valid unless the will makes it clear that your former husband intended it to remain effective after your divorce. If your former husband re-married, any will he made before his remarriage is automatically cancelled; and if he failed to make a new will, his second wife will be entitled to administer his estate.

Who else has a right to inherit?

The rules set out above are not necessarily final. Whatever the will may say or whatever the effect of the intestacy rules may be, certain people may apply to the Court for financial provision from your husband's estate. They may do so if they feel that the estate does not make reasonable financial provision for them. You may do this yourself if your husband has made a will under which you do not receive a proper share of the estate, and so may a former wife of your husband who has not remarried. Children, including illegitimate children, may also apply and so may anyone who was financially maintained by your husband, including a mistress.

The application must be made to the Court within six months of probate or Letters of Administration being granted. The Court can order that a lump sum be paid out of the estate or that regular payments are made. In reaching its decision the Court must consider the needs of the applicant and of the beneficiaries together with your husband's obligations towards the applicant and the beneficiaries; the size of the estate is also relevant as is any disability on the part of the applicant or the beneficiaries. Finally, the Court will take into account the applicant's conduct.

If you apply, the Court will consider your age, the length of the marriage and the contribution you made to the welfare of the family. The Court will bear in mind what provision you might have received if instead of your husband dying there had been a divorce. The Court will also consider any reason given by your husband (for example, in his will) for not making any provision for you. If you wish to make a claim for financial provision you should take advice from a solicitor.

Claiming compensation

If you think that you are entitled to compensation because of the circumstances of your husband's death (this will be particularly true if he has died as a result of an accident) you should consult a solicitor. It may be important to do this quickly in case vital evidence needs to be inspected before it disappears. If your husband was a union member and died as a result of an injury or disease contracted at work, the union may instruct its solicitor to act for you. Do not delay seeking advice because there is a limited time allowed in which to bring a claim for damages.

Making your own will

Your experiences may well lead you to decide that you should now make a will. If so, you should consult a solicitor. Even if you are not eligible for help with meeting legal costs, the charge is unlikely to exceed £20; and you may feel that it is worth paying this to obtain peace of mind.

Help with legal advice and costs

If you need to consult a solicitor after your husband's death, either in connection with the estate or with other matters (such as housing problems, hire purchase, consumer problems) then you may be able to get help free or at a nominal or reduced cost.

The fixed fee interview scheme provides for a solicitor to give up to half an hour of legal advice for £5 or less. This is a scheme you can use even if you have a very high income.

Legal advice and assistance (commonly known as the green form scheme) can be given for all types of solicitor's work, except Court and most tribunal representation; whether you will have to pay anything, and if so how much, depends on your income and capital. If you are entitled, a solicitor can initially do work up to the value of £50 and may be able to do more with permission from the Law Society. Get a list of solicitors who participate in the scheme from the CAB or the Law Society (address on page 103).

Legal aid is available for civil and criminal court proceedings and whether you would have to pay any costs depends on your income and capital. Unfortunately, you do not have to be very rich to find that you are outside the scope of the green form legal aid schemes. However, it should never cost anything to ask a solicitor to find out whether you are eligible. You could also look at the leaflets *Legal Aid Guide* and *Legal Aid – Financial Limits,* available from the CAB, public libraries, the courts and police stations.

Money to Live On

Ann Stanyer guides you through the maze of State benefits to help you claim your entitlement.

Most widows are entitled to receive a basic weekly income from the State – you are unlikely to have to work or depend on your family in order to survive. Many widows also receive income from private insurance and pension schemes. Private schemes vary so much that we are not going to attempt to summarise what is available.

We hope that this chapter will help to ensure that you receive what you and your husband earned through paying national insurance contributions and taxes. Many widows, especially older ones, do not claim all that they are entitled to, and this can cause unnecessary worry and difficulties.

Although we concentrate on State pensions, widows benefits and supplementary benefit, there are other benefits to which you may also be entitled, and we refer to some of these at the end of the chapter.* If you want to find out more, you can get free leaflets from the DHSS, particularly *Which Benefit?* (see page 108); and *Your Rights,* also published by Age Concern England (see page 110) describes in detail the procedures for claiming the various benefits.

The social security benefits outlined in this chapter are all provided through the Department of Health and Social Security – the DHSS. If you do not know where your local DHSS office is, then look in a telephone directory (under Health and Social Security) or ask at your nearest post office.

The rates at which these benefits are paid are increased each year. The amount you will receive from the retirement pension or widows benefits schemes depends mainly upon the national insurance contributions which have been paid by your husband (and perhaps by you if

---

* At the time of writing the Government has published its plans to make changes to this part of the 'income maintenance' system – see pages 56 – 8 for more detail of the proposals, due to start to come into effect in 1987.

you have worked in the past). Whether you are entitled to a retirement pension or one of the widows benefits depends on a number of factors, including, in particular, your age and whether you have dependent children. Your entitlement to supplementary benefit depends mainly on your income.

If you were 60 or over when your husband died, or if your husband was drawing his retirement pension when he died, you will probably be covered by the retirement pension scheme (and possibly the supplementary pension scheme which is discussed later in this chapter). But if your husband had not been entitled to retirement pension (if, for example, he was under 65 when he died) then you may be entitled to widows benefits discussed below.

The retirement pension scheme*

If you are over 60 and have already been getting a retirement pension based on your husband's contributions, you have to notify the DHSS of your husband's death so that the amount payable can be adjusted accordingly. You will find details of how to do this in your pension book or in the notes for guidance about being paid monthly or quarterly.

If you are already drawing a retirement pension based on your own contributions, but a pension based upon your husband's contributions would be higher, then your pension can be replaced by one based on his contributions. The DHSS will calculate which would be higher. If you have dependent children, you can claim increases of benefit for them.

Contributions may also have been paid into the graduated pension scheme (between 1961 and 1975) and into the additional pension scheme (which started to take effect in 1978 and is known as SERPS – the State Earnings Related Pension Scheme). Also, if retirement was deferred, additional amounts may have been earned. If your husband worked for an employer who 'contracted out' after 1978 you may have to claim your entitlement to additional pension from his employer rather than the DHSS.

You should note that if you are between 60 and 65, you cannot get a retirement pension if you work full time. The DHSS has no clear and simple rule as to what it means to be in full-time employment; but if you work only occasionally, or normally don't work more than 12 hours a week, or normally earn less than £75 a week (after taking away certain work expenses like bus fares) then you should get a retirement pension. If you do earn £75 or more in a week, your pension will be reduced because of the 'earnings rule'. But if you have been getting a widow's pension, your retirement pension cannot be reduced below the level of your widow's pension. If you earn enough you could find that you lose entitlement to your pension for that week (or it may be weeks) completely.

When you reach the age of 65, you can work and earn as much as you like without your retirement pension being affected. But you should also be aware that a retirement pension is taken into account for income tax purposes – just like any earnings you may have. We look at this in more detail in the chapter on income tax.

Claiming your retirement pension

You should claim your retirement pension within three months of becoming eligible for it – otherwise you may lose the money for the period from the date you became entitled up to the date you put in your claim. So you should fill in your claim form as soon as you receive it, even if you intend to carry on working.

If you defer retirement, bear in mind that the DHSS expect you to claim your pension four months in advance of the date you intend to retire or three months in advance of your 65th birthday – whichever is the sooner. This should give the DHSS time to have your pension ready for collection when you retire.

Widows benefits*

Widow's allowance may be payable during the first 26 weeks of bereavement if you were under 60 when your husband died, or if you were aged between 60 and 65 but your husband was not entitled to a retirement pension.

Widowed mother's allowance or a **widow's pension** may be payable after the first 26 weeks of bereavement until you reach 60 or retire. You may be entitled to a widowed mother's allowance if you have a child or children to support or to a widow's pension provided that you were 40 or over either when your husband died or after your entitlement to widowed mother's allowance ends.

If you were under 40 when your husband died, or when your entitlement to widowed mother's allowance ended, you will not be entitled to any widow's pension at all; you will cease to get any benefit 'as of right'. However, you may be able to claim supplementary benefit which is discussed later in this chapter.

---

* At the time of writing the Government has published its plans to make changes to this part of the 'income maintenance' system – see pages 56 – 8 for more detail of the proposals, due to start to come into effect in 1987.

If you are entitled to a widow's pension, then the amount you will receive is affected by your age when you become entitled to it. For entitlement to the 'standard rate' of widow's pension you must have been over 50 when your husband died, or when your entitlement to widowed mother's allowance ceased. (The standard rate of widow's pension is lower than the rate paid during the first 26 weeks of widowhood.) If you were between 40 and 50 when your husband died, or when your entitlement to widowed mother's allowance ceased, then you will receive an 'age-related' widow's pension. The amount of age-related pension is determined by a scale – the younger you are, the lower your pension. The reasoning behind this appears to be that the younger you are, the more likely you are to be able to get a job or train for a job!

When you reach pensionable age, you will be eligible to receive a retirement pension at the same rate as your widow's pension. If you have been drawing an age-related widow's pension, then you may have earned a higher rate of retirement pension if you have worked and paid national insurance contributions.

You will lose your entitlement to widows benefits if you remarry or if you live with a man as his wife. Widows benefits count as taxable income but they are not reduced or withdrawn if you choose to work. (However, a retirement pension is not affected on remarriage.)

If you were separated at the time of your husband's death, you will be treated as a widow and entitled to claim provided your husband paid sufficient national insurance contributions.

If you were divorced or your marriage was annulled, you are not entitled to draw widow's benefit. However, if you have not remarried and you have a child for whom your ex-husband paid maintenance then you may be entitled to a child's special allowance.

Industrial death benefit may be payable if your husband's death was due to an industrial accident or disease. If, at the time of making your claim for widow's benefits, you know that the cause of death was due to an industrial accident or a 'prescribed disease' (such as pneumoconiosis) then you answer 'yes' to the question about this on the BW1 form. You should also send the full death certificate issued by the registrar, because this states the cause of death.

Sometimes attributing a death to an industrial accident or a 'prescribed disease' may be thought of long after the death. If you think that your husband's death may have been caused by an industrial accident or disease, it is never too late to claim. This is not to say that establishing the cause of a death is easy – indeed you would probably need the help of a solicitor, perhaps a solicitor from your husband's trade union, to be able to make a successful claim. But each year new prescribed industrial diseases are added to the list of those recognised officially as being caused by work situations – for example, asbestosis has only relatively recently become recognised. Also evidence about an industrial accident may arise years after the event.

To repeat, if you have any reason to believe that your husband may have died as a result of an industrial disease or accident, it is worth raising the question at your local DHSS office. The level of benefit is higher than the standard widow's pension and no special national insurance contribution conditions have to be met; thus, you have nothing to lose but the time you spend investigating.

Claiming widows benefits

To claim widows benefits you can obtain form BW1 either by applying for it on form BD8 (the Certificate of Registration of Death) or by going to your local DHSS office. Although form BW1 may look large and forbidding, it is, in fact, quite easy to complete. If you wish to claim a widow's pension under the industrial injuries scheme, you should also complete form BW1.

It is quite likely at the time of completing the form you will not have all of the required information and documents to hand and where relevant you should simply indicate 'don't know' or 'I will send this on later'. **Do not delay** in submitting the form for lack of information or documents. Also do note that the staff of the DHSS office will help you complete the form, especially if you are in doubt because you do not have all of the information being requested.

The main reasons why we urge you not to delay in making your claim are that it always takes the DHSS some time to check their records and they have very strict rules about late claims. You have to claim within three months of your husband's death. If you submit your application later than this, it is possible you will never get the money owing to you from the date of your husband's death. To be successful you must show what is known as 'good cause' for a late claim; for example, if your husband had been missing for a long period and his death was not established until later, the DHSS would, of course, accept what would technically be a late claim.

Mrs Smith's husband died from asbestosis; and six months after applying for a pension under the industrial death benefit scheme she received a letter stating that unless she sent a copy of the death certificate within two weeks – they (the DHSS) would presume that she only wished to claim an ordinary widow's pension. As the inquest had not yet been held, she appealed and was given extra time to provide the death certificate.

Your entitlement to benefit starts not from the day you claim but from the day you became widowed, so when you receive your first payment, the amount will include benefit for the weeks between when your husband died and the date of the payment to you. Sometimes pensions come through very quickly – within a week or so; but sometimes widows are kept waiting several months for their pension to be sorted out. If this happens to you and you have no money to live on, you may be entitled to claim supplementary benefit to tide you over. Any supplementary benefit you do receive will be deducted from the amount of pension due when your pension is paid.

Choosing between a widow's or a retirement pension

If you are aged between 60 and 65, you may have the choice between drawing a widow's or a retirement pension – if you were receiving a widow's benefit when you reached the age of 60. If you do have this choice, then your decision will probably depend of whether you intend to work and, if so, whether you receive a full or age-related widow's pension.

If you work or intend to work while you are between the age of 60 and 65, under the special provisions of the earnings rule, you cannot be left with less than the value of your widow's pension. So it does not normally make very much difference whether you change to a retirement pension or not.

But if you receive an age-related pension, and enough insurance contributions have been made to entitle you to a standard rate of retirement pension, then you might be better off by changing. If you continue to claim your age-related widow's pension until you reach 65, you will earn extra on your retirement pension – because you will be deferring retirement. Whether it will prove financially worthwhile, in the long run, to defer your retirement depends on how long you live *after reaching the age of 65,* (and of course if you do not live that long, then you will have lost out!).

Methods of payment

If you qualify for one of the above benefits, you will normally receive a book of weekly orders which you can cash at a post office of your choice. Each order is valid for three months, and you should try to ensure that you cash it within that time; if you do not cash an order within three months, then you can apply for a replacement order. If you fail to cash an order within twelve months of the date stated, you will lose entitlement to cash it. Do also remember that you can authorise someone else to collect your pension if you cannot get to the post office.

You may also be able to be paid monthly or quarterly instead. However, you should be aware that such payments are made 'in arrears', and therefore there is no financial advantage in choosing these methods. But if you do find this more convenient, then you have to complete the application form in the national insurance leaflet NI 105 (obtainable from any local office of the DHSS). You will then receive your benefit in the form of crossed orders, valid for three months and payable directly into a bank or building society account.

Are you getting the correct amount?

If you are refused benefit or if you are awarded a weekly amount at less than you think is correct, you can ask for a check to be made and, if necessary, appeal to a social security tribunal. We know that many widows, especially elderly widows, do not like the idea of appealing. But it is important to remember that the DHSS staff are very over-worked; they do sometimes make mistakes, and they may not have received all the information they need from you to be sure that you get the right amount of benefit. The appeals system is free and is there to be used. We describe how to appeal in the chapter *'Appealing for Your Rights'*.

War widow's pension

A separate scheme covers war widows. The war widow's pension is payable at a higher rate than the ordinary widow's benefit. If your husband was, or ever had been, in the armed forces and his death could be attributed to his military service, then you may be entitled to a war widow's pension. This pension is tax free. You can receive a retirement pension in your own right as well as your war widow's pension.

If you think that you may have a claim, write to the DHSS, Norcross, Blackpool FY5 3TA giving details of your husband's service and the circumstances of his death and ask for leaflet MPL 151. Entitlement to a war widow's pension is not always straightforward, as shown in the following example.

Mrs Walsh's first husband died during the war, and she relinquished her war widow's pension when she remarried at the age of 55. Her second husband had served in the Royal Artillery for 28 years and had a good retirement pension. He died at the age of 77 when she was 72.

She was not entitled to a war widow's pension because they had married after he had come out of service.

Supplementary benefit*

Many widows receive supplementary benefit in addition to their retirement pension or widow's benefit; for some it is their only source of income. If you are entitled and 60 or over, then you will get a supplementary pension; if you are under 60, you will get a supplementary allowance.

Supplementary benefit is payable as of right if you do not work full-time, have no more than £3,000 capital and if your income is less than a minimum amount decided by Parliament each year. Working out whether you are entitled and how much you are entitled to is far from being straightforward. You should seek expert advice – either direct from the DHSS, or from a Citizens' Advice Bureau or similar local advice centre.

Usually you will be considered to be working full-time if you work for 30 hours a week or more (the rule is rather different from the rule used to decide whether you have retired or not!). If the hours you work vary, then it is worth taking advice from the DHSS; there may be some weeks when you are entitled to supplementary benefit and some weeks when you are not.

Deciding what should be counted as capital is not straightforward. We give some examples here but have not listed all the items which should be ignored or the way items should be counted. The following do not count as capital: the value of your home; personal possessions such as a car, a fur coat or jewellery; savings you have made to cover regular bills for personal living costs (such as for your heating and rent bills); the first £1,500 surrender value of insurance policies; the proceeds of the sale of your home will not usually count if you are using them to buy another home, nor will money borrowed to do essential repairs.

---

* At the time of writing the Government has published its plans to make changes to this part of the 'income maintenance' system – see pages 56 – 8 for more detail of the proposals, due to start to come into effect in 1987.

How much supplementary benefit you will get (if any) depends mainly upon your weekly income (you may have none), your housing costs (other than those covered by the housing benefit scheme discussed in the chapter *'Keeping and Maintaining Your Home'*) and on the number of your dependants. If you do find that you are entitled to weekly supplementary benefit, then you will automatically be entitled to a range of other benefits – particularly grants for certain essential items and some health benefits.

Your retirement or widow's pension counts in full as income; but housing benefit, and mobility allowance do not. Income from earnings (after deducting work expenses), income from an occupational pension scheme and part of your income from subletting also count. You should get advice on how much of your income you have to count.

When you have worked out your income, you have also to work out what your weekly needs are; if your needs are greater than your income, you will get supplementary benefit; if your income is greater than your needs, then you are not entitled. Work out your needs by finding out the current weekly scale rates for living expenses (laid down by Parliament and reviewed each year) and adding on any special weekly additions to which you may be entitled – for heating, for a special diet or laundry expenses. Get a free leaflet on supplementary benefit from your local DHSS office or post office (see list on pages 106 – 7). If you have been receiving supplementary benefit for a year or more or if you are over 60, then the weekly basic scale rate is nearly the same as the standard rate for a pension.

Mrs Jones was 72. She suffered from arthritis and her doctor recommended that she keep warm – indeed he recommended that she kept both her living room and bedroom at 70 degrees. She simply could not afford this on her pension (which was topped up by supplementary benefit). Her social worker helped her to get an extra £5.45 a week in supplementary pension (the heating allowance in November 1985). The social worker arranged for the doctor to provide a medical note for the DHSS and persuaded the DHSS to call and inspect Mrs Jones' home.

Other examples of special expenses which might be allowed are: maintenance, insurance and repair costs if you own your own home, furniture storage charges (for good reasons); and fares to visit a relative in hospital.

Special payments*

Staff at the DHSS also have the power to make single payments which are lump sum grants to meet an exceptional need. To be eligible you must not have more than £500 left after paying for the item(s) needed. Payments cannot usually be made for clothing or shoes. Most commonly, payments are made for bedding and the replacement of essential furniture. Grants can also be given for household equipment, curtains, floor covering, a cooker, heaters, an iron, a fire-guard, a hot water cylinder jacket and numerous other items. Normally a grant is intended to cover the cost of a new item although grants for furniture and household items – such as a cooker – will only cover purchase at a second-hand shop.

Mrs Finch was 62. She lived in a council house and had been widowed for seven years. She had not decorated her home since her husband died and wanted paint and wallpaper to redecorate those parts of her home which were shabbiest. Initially she did not get a grant for her redecoration costs but then made a successful appeal to a tribunal.

Claiming supplementary benefit

Claims for supplementary benefit can be made very easily by using the application form on the leaflet SB1 which you can get from a post office or the local social security office. Many younger widows do not qualify when receiving widow's allowance but become eligible when the widow's benefit changes to widow's pension or widowed mother's allowance after the first six months of bereavement. If you are refused benefit when you think you are entitled, it may be worth reapplying or perhaps appealing. (For details of how to do this see the chapter *'Appealing for Your Rights'*).

If you qualify for weekly benefit, you will normally receive a book of weekly orders which you can cash at a post office of your choice. Sometimes the DHSS will make payments by a giro order which you can cash at the post office. Single payments are usually made by a giro order which you can also cash at your local post office: in the case of a grant for furniture the DHSS may give you a voucher to use at a shop selling second-hand goods.

---

* At the time of writing the Government has published its plans to make changes to this part of the 'income maintenance' system – see pages 56 – 8 for more detail of the proposals, due to start to come into effect in 1987.

Supplementary benefit as a passport to other benefits

If you are entitled to supplementary benefit, you will automatically become entitled to free prescriptions, free dental treatment, dentures and help with paying for glasses, fares for attending hospital clinics, items supplied through the hospital such as fabric supports, and free legal aid and advice.

Other social security benefits

There are quite a lot of other social security benefits and you may be entitled to one or more of these in addition to your pension or supplementary benefit. Here are two examples.

Attendance allowance

If you are severely disabled and need someone to help look after you, then you may be able to get an attendance allowance. There are two rates at which attendance allowance is paid – a higher rate if care is needed both by day and by night and a lower rate if care is needed only by day or by night. There is no upper age limit for entitlement, but the allowance is only payable from six months after the disability has been severe enough for there to be entitlement to the benefit.

You do not need to have paid national insurance contributions to get this benefit and it does not matter how high your income is. It is not counted as income if you claim housing benefit, or if you claim a supplementary pension and live at home. But it is counted as income if you apply for supplementary pension to help pay fees in a residential care or nursing home. Attendance allowance counts as income for tax purposes.

For you to get this allowance doctors will have to be sure that you cannot manage without help – and this means, for example, needing help to move about, to use the toilet and to eat. Sometimes people don't get attendance allowance the first time they apply – and should this happen to you remember that you can re-apply or even appeal if you think you are entitled.

Invalid care allowance

If you care for someone who has an attendance allowance and cannot work because they need looking after at least 35 hours a week, you may be able to claim invalid care allowance for yourself.

Mobility allowance

Mobility allowance is a benefit to help you with getting out and about. If you are unable to walk, or virtually unable to walk, then you may be entitled. It is a benefit you could use to help run a car or to pay for taxis. To get this benefit, you must claim before you reach 66, and it ceases when you reach 75.

Mrs Vickers had become disabled many years before her husband died and long before she was 65. While her husband was alive she did not think that she would be eligible for a mobility allowance because her husband was very active and helped her to get about. But when he died her situation was very different. Unless a kind neighbour took her out she was housebound. A friend encouraged her to apply for the allowance. By this time she was 67. The DHSS refused to make an award. Had she claimed while her husband was alive, she would have received the benefit.

Proposals to reform the social security system

At the time of writing this book the Government has proposed changes in the social security system. An outline of the proposals is given in the White Paper *Reform of Social Security; Programme for Action,* published by HMSO in December 1985. There is still uncertainty about the details and the earliest of the changes are not due to come into effect until 1987; therefore we have not referred to the proposals in the main part of the book.

The Government intends to simplify the social security system and to make it easier to understand. Some of the proposals are unlikely to affect you at all; for example, the changes to the present arrangements for providing State pensions (known as SERPS) will only apply to those retiring in the next century. We concentrate here on identifying those proposals which are most likely to affect you.

If you have a low income

Income Support – if you are not in full time work – will replace the supplementary benefit system. The main difference between supplementary benefit and income support is that the latter will provide only for your basic weekly income: special needs, currently provided for by supplementary benefit single payments, will be covered by a new scheme – the social fund (see below). At present you cannot get supplementary benefit if you have £3,000 or more of savings; you may be able to get income support if you have savings of up to £6,000, provided your income is below a level to be laid down by Parliament each year. If you are an owner-occupier with a mortgage, then it is possible that only a proportion of the interest on your mortgage will be met (rather than the full amount that is usually met at present).

Family credit – if you are in full-time work and have a child or children – will replace the Family Income Scheme. The credit will top up low wages and be paid through the wage packet. The level of 'credits' will be such that you should be better off working than when on income support (many currently claiming FIS could get more income by not working and by claiming supplementary benefit instead).

The social fund – for help with exceptional needs – will replace supplementary benefit single payments. No one will have a right to grants for things like bedding and furniture or funeral costs. Grants and loans for special needs will be given from the social fund at the discretion of specially trained DHSS staff. Savings above £500 will be taken into account in deciding how much help you can get.

As the death grant (currently £30) is to be abolished, and you are responsible for the cost of a funeral, you may be able to get a grant from the social fund. If you are receiving income support or housing benefit (or family credit, if you have a dependent child or children) you will be eligible. The £1,000 lump sum payment for widows (see below) will not count as savings when determining whether you are eligible for help with funeral expenses. The amount you get will be for 'reasonable' funeral costs – like those currently allowed for in single payments under the supplementary benefit scheme.

Housing benefit – which gives help towards the cost of rent and rates – is to be simplified. One consequence of the less-complex means test is that you may find that your rate of housing benefit will be reduced. Everyone will be expected to pay at least 20% of their rates (at present some people get the whole of their housing benefit costs met).

Widows benefits

A lump sum – of £1,000 and tax free – will replace the widow's allowance (currently paid during the first six months of widowhood if you are under 60 or your husband was not retired when he died).

Widowed mother's allowance or **widow's pension** – will be payable from the time of bereavement if you were 55 or over when your husband died or you ceased to have dependent children (currently entitlement starts when you are 50).

Age related widow's pension – will be payable if you were 45 or over when your husband died or you ceased to have dependent children (currently entitlement starts when you are 40).

No widow's pension – will be payable if you were either widowed under the age of 45 or ceased to have dependent children before you reached the age of 45.

The industrial death benefit – provisions are expected to be based on similar principles to those that apply to the other widows benefits outlined above.

Keeping and Maintaining Your Home

June Hemer and Ann Stanyer outline your options — whether to stay put or to move.

For many of you the initial desolation of losing your husband will have been made worse by worries about your home. Will you be able to afford to keep it? Where will the money for the mortgage or the rent come from? Will you be able to keep it in good repair? Will you be able to keep it reasonably furnished? Will you be able to bear living in it with all its memories? What will happen as you get older and perhaps need special accommodation?

You may experience, or have experienced, a great surge of terror, of feeling overwhelmed by the immensity of the task of maintaining and retaining what has been your family home. For many widows this feeling of panic leads to decisions being taken which may result in disaster. Many recently-bereaved widows move to a smaller house or flat, move to a retirement spot by the sea or in the country and most regret such a decision. The regret comes from the strangeness of surroundings which emphasises the loneliness; from the loss of casual meetings with an old friend or shopkeeper; from the lack of support which is so often needed during the, sometimes long, period of grieving.

Roots laid down in married life are valuable; memories and possessions should not be discarded too rapidly or readily; there is help available to enable you to continue to live in the home that you and your husband built together. There is help available to enable you to move, if you want to, when you are ready . . . but not too soon. Relatives may urge you to move; they may think that you would fare best somewhere smaller. They may have your interests at heart but they may not know what is for the best.

In this chapter we look at the options that are open to you – whether you own your home or whether you rent. There are a lot of options – so if you are thinking of moving, do read this chapter first. If you own your home, then read on; if you rent your home, then turn to page 65. The sections from page 66 onwards apply both to owner-occupiers and tenants.

If you own your home

If your husband left no will or if his will is invalid, then you will be entitled to succeed to some or all of his property and you will be able to ask that the home be transferred to your name. If your husband did leave a valid will in which the home was left to someone else, then you will have to ask the court to make 'reasonable provision' for you from your husband's estate. Your solicitor will help you to do this.

Where your husband has left your family home to you in his will, you should be in a very secure position provided that his estate is solvent and either there is a mortgage protection policy or you can afford to keep up the mortgage repayments, if the property is mortgaged.

If your husband left debts and no other property from which the debts can be paid, it may be necessary to sell the house in order to pay them. If you think that this might be the case then contact a solicitor or Citizens Advice Bureau.

Many mortgages are protected by an insurance policy which means that the mortgage debt will either automatically have been paid off on your husband's death or that there is a sum of insurance money set aside for this purpose; thus, the ownership of your home should be automatically transferred to you. If there is no such insurance policy, then you may find that, in order to stay in the home, you will have to find enough money to continue the mortgage repayments.

If you have a mortgage

If you think you will have difficulty in finding enough money to keep up the mortgage repayments, then you will certainly find helpful the small book *Rights Guide for Home Owners,* published by SHAC (see page 110). This gives practical information on how to keep a home by cutting mortgage costs and increasing your income.

If you think you have no hope of finding the monthly amount needed, you will find that most lenders will prefer to adjust the amount of the monthly repayment rather than evict you. There are a number of ways in which the amount to be repaid each month can be reduced – but it may be up to you to make suggestions. Your lender is not likely to know enough of your circumstances to make suggestions to you.

The sort of proposal you make depends on what type of mortage you have. There are two main types of mortgage – capital repayment and endowment mortgages. If you are not sure which type you have, ask a relative, friend, or Citizens Advice Bureau to look at your documents.

If you have a capital repayment mortgage (building society and local authority mortgages are usually of this type) then you may be able to pay the lender just enough to cover the interest or extend the period over which the mortgage should be repaid. The longer your mortgage has been effective, the lower the interest is likely to be; and thus you could actually have very low monthly outgoings on your mortgage.

Mrs Simpson's husband had not retired when he died; their mortgage had four years to run. Her income was a retirement pension and supplementary pension. She found that she could get the interest part of the mortgage repayments covered by her supplementary benefit and thus was able to ask the building society to accept 'interest only' payments while she sorted out her finances generally.

If you see your financial difficulties as being longstanding or permanent, then you would probably be best advised to ask for a short period of paying interest only, followed by repayments over 'an extended term'. This would mean that you would take longer to pay off the mortgage but, because you are given longer to pay, the amount required each month will be lower.

If you have an endowment mortgage, then you may be able to change to a capital repayment mortgage – endowment mortgages usually cost more each month. However, the proportion of capital to interest stays constant throughout the period over which the money is lent; and if you pay tax, you might just be better off overall trying to keep the endowment mortgage. Do ask for advice on this.

Do you qualify for housing benefit? *

You may qualify for housing benefit in the form of a rate rebate; or, if you already had a rate rebate before your husband died, then you may now qualify for an increase in rate rebate.

Many younger widows do not qualify when they are receiving widow's allowance but become eligible after six months when the benefit changes to the lower widowed mother's allowance or widow's pension. Entitlement to a rate rebate means that you will pay less in general rates (not water and sewerage rates, unfortunately). You should

---

* At the time of writing the Government has published its plans to make changes to this part of the 'income maintenance' system – see pages 56 – 8 for more detail of the proposals, due to start to come into effect in 1987.

enquire about a rebate – and get the application form – from your local housing or treasurer's department.

Entitlement usually dates from when you apply but claims can be backdated for up to one year if the circumstances are exceptional – and bereavement may be accepted as exceptional because everyone knows that it takes a while to adjust to living without a husband.

Even if you do not have all the information the application form requires, do not delay in claiming. You can indicate on the form that you will send details on as soon as possible – for example, pay slips or savings. Sometimes local councils take a very long time to work out entitlement to rate rebates; and if this happens you have every right to complain, perhaps in the first instance through your local councillor.

Can you increase your income?

If you are not working or are working less than 30 hours a week, you may become eligible for supplementary benefit. If you have to depend on supplementary benefit for some or all of your weekly income, this does not mean that you will have to give up your home. Supplementary benefit can be a very stable form of income and normally increases once a year. As illustrated by Mrs Simpson's case above, you will be able to get enough to pay the interest part of your mortgage. Obviously, if your mortgage is longstanding and is a capital repayment mortgage, then the amount of interest (rather than capital) that you pay may be very small. You will need to find the money to pay the capital part of the mortgage (unless you have asked your lender to take 'interest only' for a while).

You might find that taking in lodgers helps. The amount lodgers pay over and above amounts specified by law are ignored by the DHSS and thus increase your income. If you let a room, then part of the rent you receive will be treated as income and your entitlement to supplementary benefit will be reduced. However, a portion of the profit from letting is ignored by the DHSS. Do make sure that you inform the DHSS if you decide to take in lodgers.

Maintaining your home

Your local council has a number of schemes for helping owners (this means owner-occupiers and landlords) to maintain their property. You may be able to take advantage of one or more of these – though bear in mind that sometimes the council is short of money and you may need to apply several times before being successful.

The council may be able to give you a repair grant if your home was built before 1919 and the repairs required are substantial and structural.

Examples of circumstances in which a repair grant may be given are for repairing a roof or attending to the foundations or damp caused by the structure of the house.

The council has to give you a grant (although there are plans to change this) if your home does not have and has never had, a fixed bath, a wash hand basin, a sink and hot and cold water supply. There are now not many homes left which do not have these amenities but most of those which do lack these are occupied by older people. Of course, it becomes more difficult to manage without these things the older we get.

Your council may give you a grant to cover the cost of materials for loft insulation, lagging of pipes and the insulation of hot water tanks – provided these have never been put in your home and provided you want them. This insulation can make a lot of difference to heating bills and general comfort.

You may even be able to think about improving your home. Improvement grants are given (when councils have the money) towards the cost of improvements such as putting in a damp course, extending a bathroom or kitchen, and rewiring. If you get an improvement grant, some money can be included for repairs – perhaps for fixing loose or warped window frames, for example.

The amount of, and proportion of the work covered by, the grant varies according to the work to be done and the area where you live. The amount of a grant can also depend on your financial circumstances and the attitude of the council to preventing 'hardship'. This means that, in some areas, you may get the maximum grant allowed if you are on supplementary benefit or if you have an income not much above supplementary benefit level. Also, the council may give you a loan at reasonable interest rates to help cover whatever part of the cost you have to finance.

If you can't get a council grant

You may be able to extend your mortgage or get a loan through a bank or the council to finance repairs and improvements. Often the cheapest way to do this is to extend your mortgage or, if you do not already have a mortgage, to get one.

If you are receiving supplementary benefit, the DHSS will increase your benefit to cover the interest payable on a loan, provided it seems reasonable to carry out the work. The DHSS may also finance the cost of survey fees you have to pay in connection with arranging the loan.

If you are not receiving supplementary benefit, then you will have to make sure that your income will cover the cost of increased outgoings.

If you cannot get a loan but are claiming supplementary benefit, you may be able to get a small repairs grant from the DHSS*. But, to get such a grant you have to prove that the repairs are essential to keep your home habitable.

Dealing with builders

Whatever work you decide needs doing to your home, be sure you employ a reputable contractor. Use a firm that has been recommended by someone you trust and ask to see an example of previous work.

If you are not satisfied with the job once it has been completed, and the firm refuses to meet your requirements, it might be worth seeking legal advice, although you don't want to end up paying solicitor's fees unless you have to. Your local CAB will advise you as to whether your complaint is justified and, if so, what action to take.

Using your home to raise cash

You may be able to use your home as security for a loan from a finance company, such as a building society. This kind of loan, known as a second mortgage, is particularly useful if you find yourself in the position of having to buy something that involves a large amount of money such as a car.

The amount you can borrow, the rate of interest, and the amount of time you have to repay these loans varies from one finance company to another, so make sure you shop around before you come to any final decisions. Be careful that you don't overcommit yourself and then later find that you can't afford the payments.

Insuring your home

You would be wise to ensure that you have an insurance policy to cover your home; in the event of fire, for example, it would be disastrous if you could not afford to repair the damage. Usually the institution granting the mortgage requires that you take out a policy to cover the structure of your home.

Such a policy can be very reassuring – for example, the cost of repairing damage due to burst pipes, the cost of replacing a washbasin which has been accidentally damaged (all too easy with the non-plastic ones if a glass bottle falls from a bathroom cabinet above!) should be covered. See page 79 for more information about insurance for owner-occupiers and those who rent.

If you rent your home

If you rent your home, it is likely that you have a 'protected' tenancy. Most privately rented and council homes are protected which means you cannot be evicted without a Court order. If you are a protected tenant, then you have the right to take over the tenancy provided you were living with your husband at the time of his death. You may have had a joint tenancy, in which case the tenancy will automatically be transferred to you. Sometimes the council might ask you to move to smaller alternative accommodation if this is appropriate to your circumstances.

If there are any problems, go to a solicitor, the CAB, a housing action group, or to a branch of the Widows' Advisory Service.

Help with rent and rates (housing benefit)*

If you think you cannot afford the rent and rates, you may be eligible for housing benefit or for an increase in housing benefit. This scheme is run by local councils for both private and council tenants. Whether you qualify depends mainly upon how much rent and rates you pay, your income, and the number of dependants that you have living with you. If you think that you may be eligible, go along to the housing department or write asking for an application form.

You should apply as soon as possible. Normally you can only receive housing benefit backdated to the week or period in which you applied. If you are working, you will need to send in pay slips; but if you do not have them to hand, do not delay your application – send them on later.

If you are receiving supplementary benefit and live in a council house, your rent and rates will be paid directly for you. If you are receiving supplementary benefit and live in privately rented accommodation, you will have to pay the landlord in full but will receive an allowance from the local council.

Lodgers and subletting

One way of easing the burden of maintaining a house or flat or of paying rent is to take in lodgers or to sublet a part of your accommodation. If you rent from the council or a housing association or similar body, you can take in lodgers without needing the agreement of your landlord – although you will need to have written consent if you want to sublet. If you rent privately, you should check with your landlord whether your

---

* At the time of writing the Government has published its plans to make changes to this part of the 'income maintenance' system – see pages 56 – 8 for more detail of the proposals, due to start to come into effect in 1987.

tenancy agreement allows subletting. Taking in lodgers or subletting can provide a welcome source of extra income, but do check with the DHSS or the council whether this would affect your widow's or supplementary pension or your housing benefit.

To find our more about letting your home, read the leaflets prepared by the Department of the Environment listed on page 106.

Buying your home

If you are a council or new town tenant, then you may have the right to buy your home, and be able to buy it at a discounted price. Get details from your local housing department or new town development corporation.

Whether you own or rent

Help with redecoration and furnishings

If you are claiming supplementary benefit and have lived in your home for at least a year, you may be entitled to help with the costs of essential redecoration in your home. You will have to show that, after meeting the costs, you would be left with less than £500 capital and that the redecoration is nothing to do with any major repair, renovation or alteration to your home. If you are awarded a grant, it can cover the cost of the materials – including, for example, paint, paper, paste and brushes. If you are claiming supplementary benefit, you may be able to get help with the cost of replacing essential items of furniture.

Another way that you can use your home to raise ready cash is by investing in a mortgage annuity scheme. Rather than selling your home to realise your assets, you mortgage it and use the loan to purchase an 'annuity' which pays the interest on the mortgage and also provides an income. See page 82 for more details.

Help for disabled widows

There are also ways in which your home could be altered or adapted to make it easier for you to cope with everyday tasks. In addition, there are domiciliary services available and special housing for disabled people. A social worker can advise.

Because facilities for the disabled is a subject that requires special consideration, we must limit ourselves to referring you to your social services and housing departments and the books and leaflets listed on pages 107 – 9.

Making your home secure

Without your husband, and possibly living alone for the first time in your life, you may feel very vulnerable. It is worth ensuring that you have good security locks fitted and perhaps a chain or a door viewer so that you can see who is at the door before opening it fully.

It is also wise to have locks fitted to accessible windows. Keeping the outside of your home well lit after dark will also deter burglars. If you are going to be away, a time switch which will automatically turn on an inside light when it gets dark will also help. It will also help if you go out in the evening to have one in the hall, because you will not have to fumble for light switches when you get in.

You could also try to ensure that it is not obvious that your home does not have a man in it. If you live in a block of flats, then you might just use your initials and surname on your letter box or door. If you have a telephone, use only your initials and surname in the directory.

The Crime Prevention Officer at the local police station will be pleased to advise you on any aspects of security which are worrying you.

Looking after appliances and plugs

One of the things you may have to learn about is how to recognise the signs of danger in your home – for example, wiring may have perished, appliances may need servicing.

Simple things like worn flexes on kettles and irons can cause disasters; flexes should be replaced by a competent electrician. The wires in plugs may become loose and should be checked regularly. New plugs come with clear instructions about correct wiring, but if your plugs or appliances are old, the colouring codes may be different and you may need to take advice. It is not easy to wire plugs especially if you have arthritic hands; you can buy ones with the wire ready stripped and this helps. But always make sure that new plugs conform to what is known as the British Standard 1363 – a kite should be on the label.

If you use adaptors to hold several plugs, then make sure that you do not overload the power point. Old wiring can cause fires and should be checked at least every five years; your electricity board can do this, and although there will be a charge, you will at least have peace of mind.

Appliances, especially colour televisions, should be unplugged (not just switched off) from the mains when not in use. Electric under-blankets should NEVER be left switched on when you are in bed.

All gas appliances should be checked regularly, preferably once a year. The gas board provides this service at a reasonable cost. Any smell of gas should be investigated immediately; first make sure there are no naked flames in your home. The gas board does prompt, free emergency checks. Gas water heaters needs special care, as there must always be an unrestricted flow of air and the flues must be kept in good repair and free of obstructions.

If you use paraffin heaters, place them where they cannot be knocked over. Keep the paraffin outside, refill heaters outside and always wipe off any spilled paraffin before you light up.

Coal fires should always be guarded, especially when you are out of the room, for fire can drop from a grate so quickly. Lighted, or only partially stubbed out, cigarettes are a well-known fire hazard and visitors' cigarettes need your vigilance.

For more information on home safety look at the booklets issued by the gas and electricity boards and write for the book *Safety in Retirement* (see page 110).

If you are considering a move

You may decide that you would like to move out of your present home, perhaps to another area to join family or friends. If you own your present home, then you can sell it and buy or rent a new home.

If you decide to buy another property, you may use an estate agent; but remember that agents take a commission. Your solicitor may not only be able to deal with the legal side of the sale and purchase but, if you need it, can also advise on financial matters, such as whether you are eligible for a mortgage.

You may want to apply for housing association or council accommodation. You should be warned that there are long waiting lists and often councils will not accept applications from people who have owned their own home or are from other areas.

If you can't afford to buy a house, then it is worth knowing about the Tenants Exchange Scheme. If you register with your local council your name will appear on a list which is sent to the housing department in the area where you wish to move. If a tenant there decides she/he would like to exchange with you, she/he will contact you directly. You can also look at the list held by your housing department to see if there are any people wanting your sort of house from the area where you want to move. You could also try to get an exchange by advertising in a local newspaper in your chosen area.

Most councils participate in the National Mobility Scheme which provides a limited number of properties for people (not just council tenants) who want to move to be near their family or for strong social reasons.

If you want to rent privately, then you could contact estate agents in your chosen area and ask to be put on their mailing list; they will send you details of properties which fit your requirements.

Special accommodation

So far in this chapter we've been considering various ways you can house yourself provided you are able to look after yourself with reasonable comfort and safety.

If you are a less active person or want to move into accommodation with communal services and/or a warden available, then you could consider sheltered housing, which is provided by housing associations, local councils and private companies. A sheltered flat or bungalow is independent accommodation with some communal facilities and usually a warden who can mobilise help in emergencies. Most sheltered housing is rented, but many housing associations and private companies now have accommodation for sale.

You can get information on local schemes from council housing departments, housing advice centres, Age Concern groups and Age Concern England. Details of sheltered housing for sale can be obtained from the New Homes Marketing Board (address on page 103); and Age Concern England has produced a useful guide on what to look out for when considering a purchase.

You may feel that a residential home is the most realistic option. These are run by social services departments and private and voluntary agencies. Standards and styles of homes vary considerably, and you should find out as much as you can about a home before accepting a place. Ask for a trial period. Charges also vary considerably but you may be eligible for help from social security or by local authority sponsorship if you are in a private or voluntary home. Details of provision can be obtained from social services departments and from Counsel and Care for the Elderly (address on page 101).

There are also nursing homes run by private and voluntary agencies that provide nursing care. You can get information on nursing homes from district health authorities, social services departments or from the Registered Nursing Home Association (address on page 104). Charges vary, but if you are on a low income you may be able to claim supplementary benefit for the board and lodging element but not for the medical fees. In a very few cases fees may be paid through an arrangement with the district health authority. Counsel and Care for the Elderly can provide information on extra sources of financial help for nursing homes.

Moving in with friends or relatives

Some people resolve their housing problems by going to live with relatives or friends who can look after them. Neither you nor your relatives, however, should feel forced into this arrangement or into selling your house by pressures either from statutory services, such as hospital doctors and social workers, or your family. If you decide to go and live with your family, make sure you and they receive all the support services and benefits to which you are entitled. The Association of Carers and the National Council for Carers and Their Elderly Dependents can advise on these matters (addresses on pages 100 and 103). Check with the DHSS that such an arrangement will not affect your supplementary or widow's pension.

Paying the Right Amount of Tax

June Hemer explains how income tax may affect you and what responsibilities you have.

Income tax is a sore point with very many people, not least widows. The Government collects taxes of various sorts in order to help to pay for many of the services from which we all benefit. Whether or not you have to pay taxes in general, and income tax in particular, depends very much on your individual circumstances. Although you are aware that you pay taxes on a lot of items, you may not know on which things VAT (Value Added Tax) is charged; therefore, even if you wanted to, it would be difficult to avoid paying tax on purchases.

Whether you have to pay income tax depends not only on the size of your income but also on where that income comes from. In the chapter *'Money to Live On'* we list the benefits that are taxable – for example, widows benefits and retirement pensions. Nevertheless, you can have taxable income like the retirement pension and yet not have to pay any tax. This is because of 'tax allowances' – a yearly amount of income on which you do not have to pay tax; you only pay tax on, income above that yearly set amount. And if your income is lower than the set amount, you do not pay any tax at all. The set amount is not just a simple figure – it is made up of what are called personal allowances and other tax allowances or tax reliefs.

The allowances are decided at Budget time, and shortly after that everyone receives a Notice of Coding which specifies what allowances are due. If you do have to pay tax then the amount you pay will depend on the 'tax rates', also decided by the Chancellor – in general, you pay more, the higher your income.

Rather than describe the tax system in detail, we suggest that you look at Age Concern's book *Your Taxes and Savings in Retirement* (see page 110) and Cruse's Fact Sheet No 2 (address on page 119) if you want to find out more. Here we discuss the sort of problems widows have with their tax matters and how to deal with them.

If you have never had to deal with income tax matters before, then be reassured that they are rarely as complicated as they are rumoured to be. Always check with the local tax office if you are not sure about anything. If you go to see, or write to, the income tax authorities as soon as possible after your husband's death, you will almost certainly avoid any major problems. It is best to do things in writing – and to keep a copy of anything you write or a record of your visits to the tax office. If you make telephone calls, then keep a note of the date and items discussed. It is possible that your only contact with the Inland Revenue will be completing a tax return.

Filling in a tax return

If you've never had to fill one in before, a tax return is a form made up of several pages on which you give details of your income and certain types of expenditures. It is this form that the Inland Revenue use to decide whether you have to pay tax at all and if so how much. For most widows it is a simple form to complete – only answer the questions that are relevant to you and leave the others blank. If you feel nervous about completing the form, then get a friend to help you or ask at the Inland Revenue office for advice.

Tax allowances for widows

Widows, including widows over retirement age, get special personal allowances. If you are over 65, then depending on the level of your income, you will get the special age allowance; regardless of your age you will get the widow's bereavement allowance which is given both in the tax year when your husband died and in the following year – this allowance (when added to the single person's allowance) is equal to the allowance your husband had as a married man. If you have dependent children, you will also be able to claim the additional personal allowance for single parents.

For widows who have an income high enough to put them into the tax paying bracket, these allowances can soften the financial blow of bereavement. The higher the value of your allowances, the less tax you will have to pay.

What counts as income for tax purposes?

The Inland Revenue publish a very useful short guide called *Income Tax and Widows* (IR 23). You will see from the leaflet that the following items of income are liable to be taxed:

widow's national insurance benefits (widow's allowance, widowed mother's allowance, widow's pension, industrial death benefit, etc.)

all other pensions and annuities (retirement pensions, pensions from your husband's employment, etc.)

wages, salaries and income from self-employment, interest, dividends, etc.

Tax-free income

If you are a war widow, then your pension and any extra pension for your children and any rent allowance do not count for income tax purposes. Other income which does not count includes supplementary benefit (unless it is paid because of unemployment), housing benefit, the Christmas bonus, invalidity pension and mobility allowance.

The tax 'threshold'

There have been times in recent years when even a widow who did not work may have had to pay tax on her widow's benefit. At the time of writing this is no longer the case, as the tax 'threshold' – the lowest level of allowances – is slightly above the amount paid in standard widow's benefit. But if you work, you will probably find that you are taxed on almost the whole of your earnings.

Keeping the Inland Revenue informed

The golden rule is always to inform the authorities of changes in your circumstances and to check that you know what demands will be made of you. If the Inland Revenue are informed of your husband's death promptly, they will make adjustments so that you should not experience problems; but if you delay in informing them about your husband's death, you may get into 'tax arrears' and receive a hefty demand from the tax collector.

When you inform the tax office that your husband has died, the inspector will ask you to estimate the amount of any benefits (pension, widow's allowance, etc.) you are likely to receive. You can get an estimate by asking at your local DHSS office. When the inspector has this information, but not before, he will try to estimate how much tax will be due up to the end of the financial year (the 5th April after the death of your husband).

If you are working, he will adjust your tax code so that by the end of the financial year you should have paid the correct amount of tax. If you are not working, the inspector will be able to tell you whether you are likely to be liable for any tax, and if so, how much it will be and how this should be paid.

Tax on your husband's income

The tax due on the period up to the date of your husband's death will have been deducted from his wages or salary if he was employed; if he was self-employed or retired, there may be tax due, and normally this will be settled by the executors when they wind up the estate.

If you have any doubts – whether your husband was employed, self-employed or retired – then contact your local inspector of taxes.

How is tax collected?

You will find that tax is not deducted directly from your widow's benefit or pension. Any tax due will be payable to the collector of taxes in one of two ways. If you are not working, or not in receipt of a taxable occupational pension, you will be asked to pay a specified amount, usually four times a year. If you are working, tax will be deducted from your wages or salary at a rate that takes into account your pension or widow's benefit. Thus a working widow receives less in her pay packet than a single or married woman doing the same job for the same money. The reason for this is that the single or married woman will not be in receipt of a taxable benefit in addition to her wages. Many widows feel that this is very unfair and that the widow's pension should be tax free. No government has yet felt able to make pensions tax free even though some tax concessions are given to war widows.

You will probably be surprised at how long it can take for the Inland Revenue to sort out your tax affairs. Some widows have approached the Widows' Advisory Service for help because they have just received their first tax demand – two years after their husband died.

If you have no money to pay your tax?

Sometimes a tax demand comes when you simply do not have the cash to pay the bill. This can easily arise if you have not been aware that tax was due on the income you have had – most widows just do not realise that their pension is taxable. When a lump sum payment is requested by the collector of taxes, you should contact him immediately and ask for extra time to pay if the amounts being requested will cause you financial hardship. By asking for extra time you may be able to pay smaller amounts on the four times during the year when your tax becomes due.

Mrs Martin lived with her son in a council house. Her income barely covered their needs, so when she received a tax demand for £70 and payment was expected immediately, this was a terrible shock to her. She had no idea that she would have to pay any tax at all and had no means of paying the bill. Arrangements were made for her to pay the debt off over a period of a year so as to cause her as little hardship as possible. From then on she was able to budget for this expense.

If you are working and have tax arrears, you may be asked to pay the tax due by having more deducted from your wages or salary each week or month than would otherwise be due. If the amount being deducted leaves you too little on which to live, ask the inspector of taxes to make an adjustment so that you can pay it off more slowly.

Paying interest on tax due

If you have underpaid tax due to the Inland Revenue because they lacked all the details they needed to make a proper assessment, you may not only have to pay what is owed but you may also be charged interest on that amount. This is another good reason for making sure that you keep the inspector of taxes informed of your financial circumstances.

Mistakes by the Inland Revenue

Sometimes staff of the Inland Revenue do, like the rest of us, make mistakes. The Inland Revenue have adopted the practice of ignoring tax arrears which arise through 'official error'. An official error means that the Inland Revenue have received information which is necessary to enable a correct assessment of tax liability to be made but that such information has not been used appropriately or within a reasonable period of time by staff of the Inland Revenue. Thus if it is established that in your case there has been an official error, you should make representation to the Inland Revenue asking that any tax arrears are not collected and any payments due you are paid, with interest.

At the time of writing the Inland Revenue are not collecting any arrears arising from official error where the gross income is less than £10,500 if you are receiving a state retirement or widow's pension. If your gross income is higher than this amount, you may have to repay part, or even all, of what is due. In practice the Inland Revenue will not try to recover arrears arising out of official error if hardship would thus be caused.

Mrs James received a tax demand for over £500. She lived in London and the demand had come from a tax office in the north of England. It was eventually discovered that the Inland Revenue had not made 'proper and timely' use of information that she had given in her tax return – information about her widow's pension, a private pension and unemployment benefit. She had in fact underpaid tax for two years. The Widows' Advisory Service made representations on her behalf and the Inland Revenue withdrew the tax demand – under the official error provisions.

What if the Inland Revenue owe you money?

If the Inland Revenue make a mistake which results in refunds being due to you – if you have been overcharged tax – then you may have a right to be paid the arrears, plus interest, provided the repayment is £25 or more and a full tax year has passed. You have a right to claim tax allowances and reliefs retrospectively for up to six years – that means that if you find you have not been receiving an allowance or a relief during the past six years, then you can make a claim and expect reimbursement.

Tax rebates

When you retire it is important to check whether you may be entitled to a tax rebate. If you are getting a pension from your employer, any tax rebate due should be paid automatically with your pension. If you get a pension paid by someone other than your last employer, then you should give them your P45 – the Certificate of Tax Deducted which should be handed to you when you finish work. If you get no pension other than your state pension, then send your P45 to your tax office, as the form gives the details necessary for deciding whether you are entitled to a rebate.

Making the Most of Your Money

June Hemer and Andrea Ufland explain how to keep your costs down, spread them evenly, and make investment plans.

The realisation that you alone must now be the one responsible for sorting out the finances is sometimes one of the biggest blows, particularly if you have never concerned yourself with money. Money in all its forms is complicated enough, but to have to make sense of dealing with it when you are at your lowest ebb makes it even more so.

Many widows are left very short of money. Some have little because they've never had much and some have little because their husbands have not taken out appropriate insurance and made other provisions to enable their wives to maintain their standard of living.

Mrs Ackroyd's husband had been a solicitor who was a partner in a practice, but he had made no provisions for her in the event of his death. When she came to the Widows' Advisory Service she was living in one room and had been forced to give up the nice flat that they had owned when he was alive.

If you are short of money

If you are short of money there are a number of things you can do to keep down your costs and to spread them evenly.

Paying gas and electricity bills

Finding the money to pay gas and electricity bills, especially during the winter months, can be difficult. It is important not to skimp on heating, because of the risk of hypothermia.

If you get supplementary benefit, you should check whether you are entitled to an extra weekly amount for heating costs and a grant for curtains to keep out the draughts. If your home is not well insulated, you should check whether you can get an insulation grant from the local council. If you do not understand how your heating system works get advice from the gas and electricity boards on the most economical way of using it.

Spreading the cost of paying heating bills evenly throughout the year can also help; you can budget with more confidence, and you will know that at the end of the twelve months if you have overpaid, you will get a rebate towards your next bill. If you have underpaid, you will only have the balance owing to find.

You make regular payments either by standing order on your bank account or by getting a book of payment slips from the electricity or gas board and paying (usually monthly) at your local showroom or post office. Alternatively you can buy savings stamps at the fuel board showrooms or at some larger post offices.

Or you could have a meter installed and pay as you consume your fuel. If you choose this method, then you have to pay for the installation of the meter. You should also take into account that meters tend to be a security risk.

It is very important to make sure that fuel bills are paid normally – if your supply is disconnected, you will have to pay a re-connection fee (and you may be asked to pay the bill in full). The electricity and gas boards do have Codes of Practice which specify that if you are a pensioner or are ill, your supplies should not be cut off between October 1st and March 31st.

If you are unable to pay a fuel bill, contact the fuel board as quickly as possible and ask to make arrangements to pay off what you owe over an extended period of time. If you get supplementary benefit, you could ask to use the 'fuel direct' scheme; an amount estimated to be enough to cover your fuel bill can be deducted from your weekly benefit, and the DHSS will then pay the electricity or gas board each quarter.

Spreading costs throughout the year

There are other costs which can also be spread evenly throughout the year – you can buy stamps at the post office for your TV licence, for telephone bills and car tax. Of course, you must keep your books of stamps in a safe place – or you could lose all the benefit of this facility.

Mail order and other credit clubs can be good ways of keeping your wardrobe replenished and of replacing worn-out household furnishings and furniture. You might even be able to earn yourself commission if you become an agent and get your friends and family to order for themselves through you. The cost of items may be more than what you would pay in major department stores, but the convenience of shopping from home and being able to budget carefully also have value.

Checking the small print in contracts

It is important to take care when signing contracts of all sorts. Make sure that you know what your rights and liabilities are. For example, one widow took out an insurance policy on a TV set and was horrified to find that when she called out the engineer she had to pay the bill herself and then send the receipt to the insurance company for re-imbursement.

Insuring your possessions

You should arrange for your personal possessions and the contents of your home to be insured. Age Concern England has a Household Contents Insurance Scheme at reasonable rates. (For details, write to the insurance office at the address on page 118.) In addition, the Standard Insurance Company has arranged an advantageous deal for house contents insurance with the National Association for Widows; and you can write for a leaflet describing the plan at the address given on page 119.

Getting value for money

Whenever you buy goods or pay for a service, you are entering into a contract with the seller. This contract gives both of you certain rights and obligations which today are well-defined in law. However, you do not have to rely solely on the law for protection. Codes of practice adopted by many trade associations give you benefit over and above your legal rights. To find out more about organisations which watch over your interests as a consumer and deal with complaints, you could buy a copy of *Fair Deal,* published by the Office of Fair Trading (see page 110.)

Too few people complain about goods which fail to perform as expected from their description or advertisements, about dirty shops or restaurants, about services which do not function adequately. By law goods have to be reasonably fit for the purpose for which they were intended; this includes both sale and second-hand goods like motor cars which you might buy through an advertisement in a local paper.

In the first instance you should complain to the person who sold you the unsatisfactory item or service. If you do not get satisfaction, then you could go to your local CAB for further advice and if the situation merited it, even through the courts. An example of the latter might be if you had central heating installed and it failed to heat your property to a reasonable temperature — perhaps because the supplier recommended radiators which were patently too small for the rooms.

If you are planning to buy an item or service, it may be worth looking at the Consumers' Association magazine *Which?* in your local library; you will find surveys of all sorts of products and services – from small household items like washing powder to expensive items like cameras and cars and services like mortgages and insurance policies – and recommendations as to the 'best buys'. *Which?* can save you time, trouble and money.

If you have money to invest

Many widows have money in bereavement for the first time in their lives. This new-found wealth does not necessarily bring the happiness that may be expected. For many widows this having money is a source of great resentment, bitterness and anger, as shown by the example below. Widows are also easy prey for salesmen, and almost as soon as the obituary notice appears, there is an insurance salesman on the doorstep. Many widows buy immediately because the offers are made to seem so attractive; others hesitate but are so harrassed that they buy in the end and then regret it later.

Mrs Jordan's husband had made her scrimp and 'go without' during their married life. He left her with a vast sum of money that she never knew he had.

Mrs Blake wrote for help, saying that she and her husband never had any money during their lives together. When he died she found that there was about £100,000 in the bank. She felt very angry towards him.

If you are fortunate enough to have been left with anything from £1,000 upwards, you can make that capital work for you, enhance your standard of living, provide protection against inflation. Remember that women live a lot longer than they used to, and usually live longer than men; what might seem like a large sum today will soon diminish if not invested properly. It is not easy to get good advice on how to make the most of any money you may have.

Getting the right advice

Many widows who are left with money decide to take the advice of a well-meaning friend or bank manager. Many plump for the easy solution of putting all the money into a bank or building society. Neither of these courses of action may be wise.

A widow was left with shares worth £7,500 which she did not want. She asked the bank to invest them for her and without even checking with her they put them into a property bond, at a time when property bonds did not give a good rate of return.

If you are dealing with a solicitor in connection with your late husband's estate, you could ask him or her to recommend an adviser. What you should make sure of is that a financial adviser is independent (as far as they can be!) and not attached to one particular financial group. A reputable insurance broker should be able to offer impartial advice on most aspects of your money – compare this advice with that suggested by your bank manager, solicitor or accountant.

Most financial advisers are men, and many widows resent the way they are treated by male advisers – they feel they can't cry in front of them; they find it very difficult to understand men, say men are patronising and often rude, and prefer to get advice from a woman.

Mrs Eden said: 'It made such a difference having a woman to talk to – I felt she understood. Not only did she give me advice but I understood what she was talking about. I also found her a great comfort. My previous experiences of trying to get advice had been awful. The men were so rude to me. They didn't have any patience.'

So it is worth trying to find a woman – perhaps through the Widows' Advisory Service – who can help you to make decisions about your money, however little or much you have. No two women have the same requirements; but it is always sensible to get professional advice, even for the smallest of assets.

If you seek advice you should expect to be told: how to invest capital wisely; how to secure a sufficient income; the implications of the tax system, especially Capital Transfer Tax, (see page 39).

Making an investment plan

It is not sufficient to look at the situation as it exists now, or to look at one aspect in isolation. It is important to take stock of your total situation and to make a plan. The key areas to cover are:

Your future intentions and ideals – your plans for your children; you may still have business interests; if you have been bereaved for some time, you may even be thinking about the possibility of marrying.

Your current financial position – your assets, liabilities, liquidity, future inheritances. You may also need to consider assets held by other members of your family.

Your tax position – your current tax return will show the yield on investments, the rates of tax you pay and the income you have available to spend.

The unexpected – an examination of your current insurance and the assets you hold to cover death, disablement, illness, and retirement if you have not retired already.

Death – what would happen to your estate on death in the absence of a will and what is the current 'exposure' to death duties.

Your investment strategy – what net spendable income do you need; what mix of income yielding and capital investments would achieve this for you.

The protection of your current position and your future, and that of your dependants if you have any, must always come first. You must protect your home, make sure you have enough to live on; you must have adequate insurance and 'liquid assets' (money you can get your hands on quickly such as in bank current and deposit accounts) for the unexpected. The balance of any resources left can then be invested to give you the best possible return.

Some options to consider

Annuities are not recommended as an investment for women under 75 years of age. But for women aged 75 and over, the rates become attractive and a lump sum can provide a tax efficient guaranteed income. However, it is not usually possible to surrender an annuity once it is purchased, and there is the risk that the payments will decrease in value due to inflation. Income from an annuity can also affect your eligibility for supplementary benefit, housing benefit (for example, rate rebate) and a range of other benefits.

A home income plan could enable you to 'unlock' capital tied up in your home, thus providing you with a tax efficient income for the rest of your life. This method of obtaining an income from capital should be used, however, only when other sources of capital have been exhausted. You may be surprised at how little income this type of scheme would give you each week and therefore you should only use a home income plan (or mortgage annuity scheme) after giving it very careful thought. With this scheme a mortgage is granted on your home by a life insurance company of which at least 90% must be invested in a purchased life annuity. On your death the money borrowed is repaid from the proceeds of the sale of the property.

An investment package or a spread of assets may be a useful option for younger women who require an income from capital. Such a 'package' could include investments in unit trusts, gilts, (possibly carefully chosen stocks and shares), guaranteed income bonds, Government income bonds, building societies and banks (not for non-tax payers). This is where planning will depend entirely on personal circumstances, but as a general rule it is wise to have some income from a stable source, like National Savings and deposit accounts.

Any investment linked to the rate of inflation must be monitored carefully because there are sometimes conditions when even deposit interest rates are three or four per cent above inflation. Index-linked gilts and index-linked National Savings are only a good choice if the inflation rate is high and interest rates are low in comparison.

The tax aspect needs to be considered carefully too, as some income-bearing investments are free of the basic rate of tax and others are not. You should always be aware of why you are paying tax so that, if possible, your affairs can be re-arranged to reduce your tax bill. It is not as difficult as it may at first appear, provided you find out which elements of your income are taxed and then see how you can adjust your position to make full use of your allowances.

With any financial planning – whether for capital growth or income – the most important step is to work out clearly in your own mind what you want from your investment. This seems a very obvious statement, but it is very easy to approach financial planning the wrong way round, by looking at a limited number of areas to put your capital and choosing one of them. A wide spread over several areas is much better and would provide the flexibility you will probably need.

Before you even begin to think about investing in areas like the stock market or unit trusts, you should first establish some fundamental points, such as, how much insurance you need, the size of your mortgage and whether or not it is wise to keep a mortgage at all and what 'liquid' savings you need to maintain. All of these points will be influenced by your age, whether you work, your family's position, your retirement date and any other special circumstances.

Your tax position

One reason why taxation is often such a worry, to widows in particular, is that your late husband's company may have dealt with his financial affairs automatically through the PAYE (pay-slip) system. In effect, free advice and administrative services were available to handle the problem. Many widows feel that their affairs are too trivial to involve an accountant, but however trivial, they still have to be dealt with and can still cause many headaches.

Capital Transfer Tax (CTT) becomes a very serious matter when one partner dies because although there is tax payable from spouse to spouse, the tax liability has only really been deferred; it becomes a very real issue for the surviving partner. The rates of CTT payable on lifetime transfers are half those payable on death. The maximum rate of CTT on lifetime gifts is 30% and therefore a maximum of 60% on death. In order to secure the lower, lifetime rates of CTT the donor must survive his gift by at least three years. If he or she dies within that period, the death rates will be substituted (see page 39).

There are trusts run by insurance companies to mitigate the financial consequences of untimely death. The savings which can be made are quite substantial and it is well worth seeking advice from an insurance broker if CTT is a potential problem. The solutions usually enable you to keep control of all your assets during your lifetime and yet still pass it on intact upon your death. Many people think that you can only secure the lifetime rates by unconditionally giving away your money, but this is not necessarily the case.

Whilst it is impractical to go into great detail due to the complexity of the subject and the fact that each person's circumstances are unique, the following types of trust can be used: lifetime trusts, accumulation trusts, discretionary trusts, Capital Transfer Tax discount schemes and inheritance trusts. Professional advice must be sought before making use of these.

Reviewing your plan

It is unfortunate that for many people financial planning is really only tackled when finances are in a mess, or when a problem has arisen to force us to look at our affairs more closely. You should also bear in mind, though, that as you get older you will be well advised to make sure that your money is easy to manage. A lot of widows, for example, have money invested in several building societies. Whilst you should not have more than between £3,000 and £4,000 in any one building society, if your total amount is up to this level, it does make sense to have the money in one place. Investments should be made simple; it should be easy for you to see what you have got and what you might have.

If at all possible, once a financial plan is set out and still hot on the press, make a promise to yourself that you will keep that plan under review. In most cases, six-monthly reviews are adequate or even annual reviews for some aspects. It is always easier to maintain a plan than to start one afresh so do not let time erode your good work and then force you to rethink the whole package again. If you take a keen interest in your financial planning, you may be surprised how much you begin to enjoy it.

Appealing for Your Rights

Ann Stanyer explores what you can do if you think that you have suffered from bad administration or a wrong decision by a public body.

Sometimes you may think that you have been treated badly or wrongly by a public authority official or department. You might, for example, have suffered an intolerable delay while waiting for your entitlement to widow's pension to be sorted out or you might be sure that you are paying too much income tax.

You have a right to expect reasonable standards of service from central and local government departments and from health authorities; in such circumstances you can complain about bad administration (often called maladministration). It may be difficult to establish your correct entitlement to benefits and your liability for income tax; appeals procedures, rather than the courts, are designed to contribute to ensuring that correct decisions are made.

Appeals to the ombudsmen

Ombudsmen exist to promote good administration. You have the right to appeal to – the Parliamentary Commissioner for Administration, the Commissioners for Local Administration or the Health Service Commissioners (who are popularly known as ombudsmen) about any matters where you think there has been maladministration. You appeal to any of the above according to whether the service you want to complain about is run by central government, local government or the health authorities.

To appeal to the Parliamentary Commissioner for Administration, make a written complaint and send it to your own MP (another MP can take your case but would not normally do so). You should send as much detail as possible and any relevant documents within 12 months of being aggrieved to your MP at the House of Commons, London SW1. The Parliamentary Commissioner will receive and investigate complaints about, for example, the DHSS, the Inland Revenue, the Department of Employment, the Department of Education and Science.

To appeal to one of the Commissioners for Local Administration, write to a local councillor who will then take the matter further. The Commissions for Local Administration deal with maladministration of services such as housing, social services, local education, planning. You can get the names of local councillors from the council's offices or from the Citizens Advice Bureau.

To appeal to a Health Service Commissioner you apply through your local Family Practitioner Committee within a year of the incident of alleged maladministration. You can find the address in the phone book, listed under the name of your local health authority. You should send all the details and any relevant documents. The type of cases dealt with include bad communications, delays in admission to hospital, inadequate facilities, and failure to deal with complaints.

Sometimes it is difficult to decide whether what you want to complain about is maladministration or another matter. For example, a widow who thinks her husband was not treated correctly by the doctor would not be able to make a complaint about maladministration: such a complaint is about professional competence and judgement and would normally be taken, in the first instance, direct to the Family Practitioner Committee.

Decisions of Commissioners rarely bring any direct benefit to the person who makes the complaint. But other people benefit substantially from improvements in procedure; one good example of this was that a hospital failed to give adequate information to a patient about claiming sickness benefit – the Commissioner's finding of maladministration resulted in the hospital giving all patients (including emergency admissions) a booklet with the necessary advice.

Appeals about income tax

You have a right to appeal about your income tax – normally within 30 days of receiving your Notice of Assessment. You can appeal either by using the form 64-7(S) which is enclosed with the assessment or by writing to the tax inspector saying that you want to appeal. You can appeal outside the normal thirty-day limit if you can give good reasons for a late appeal.

You should indicate why you are appealing and give any extra information which may be relevant. You should also pay the tax demand or apply for a postponement of payment.

Usually the tax inspector will come to an agreement with you and your appeal will not have to be heard. However, if the disagreement over your tax liability persists, then your appeal will be heard either by the General Commissioners or the Special Commissioners. Most appeals go to the General Commissioners – local non-specialists who are advised by a clerk – who hear appeals locally. There is no legal aid, so any costs you incur have to be borne by you. The Widows' Advisory Service may be able to help you to prepare your case without charge.

Appeals about social security benefit

Sometimes you may think you have been treated wrongly or unfairly by staff at the DHSS with regard to your widow's or retirement pension or perhaps supplementary benefit. You may even find that your benefit has been stopped and you may not understand why, or you may consider that the DHSS has wrongly withdrawn your benefit. In these circum-stances you have a right of appeal.

You can appeal to a local social security tribunal. Such tribunals are totally independent of the DHSS, and appeals are usually heard by three people, a chairman and two members. Appeals are informal and you should be given as much time as you wish to explain your appeal and to be heard sympathetically. The appeals tribunal system is a safeguard against mistakes being made by DHSS officials and often allows information to be presented that DHSS officials have not asked for but which is relevant to your circumstances. Tribunals exist to be used and have been used successfully by many widows.

The appeals procedure

You can appeal against any decision of an official of the DHSS. You can appeal, normally within 28 days of the decision, simply by saying that you wish to appeal against the decision to. . . (e.g. refuse benefit) taken on . . . (date) and hand this in at your local DHSS office. Common examples are as follows: appeals against refusal to award supplementary benefits or widows benefits, appeal about the amounts awarded, appeals against the withdrawal of benefits, appeals about alleged cohabitation. You will see in the examples that follow how widows have appealed and won their cases.

A week before an appeal hearing is due, you will receive the tribunal papers, which set out your reasons for appealing, the reasons why the DHSS took the original decision and the relevant law. Usually these papers come through about three weeks after you lodge an appeal about supplementary benefits and perhaps as much as three months after you lodge a national insurance appeal. Since the papers arrive only about one week before the date on which your hearing is to be heard, you will either have to think quickly in order to prepare your case or you have to ask for an adjournment – i.e., ask that the date for the hearing is postponed (you will find discussion as to when it is appropriate to do this in some of the examples that follow). The tribunal papers are very important because you will not find out the full reasons for the original decision until the papers arrive.

Many widows try to get a friend, social worker or member of the Widows' Advisory Service to help them with their case; you cannot get legal aid and therefore it is quite expensive to employ a solicitor to help you. When you receive the tribunal papers, you will see that there is a reply slip on which you indicate whether you want to be present at the hearing of your case and which enables you to say whether you intend to be represented. If you do take along a friend or social worker, then indicate that you will be represented when you complete the reply slip. You can also use the reply slip to request an adjournment if you want a little more time, perhaps to find someone to help you.

It is always important to attend your hearing or to get someone to go in your place. The members of the tribunal will otherwise make their decision on the basis of DHSS papers alone – and obviously you are not likely to win in this situation. If you attend you can explain your position, mention any relevant evidence, discuss why you think the DHSS has been wrong; in this situation you can expect a fair hearing.

You will have your expenses associated with attending the hearing reimbursed on the spot. If you work you will also have your loss or earnings reimbursed. Usually any friend, relation or volunteer who attends to help you will have his or her expenses or loss of earnings reimbursed too.

Hearings usually take place in a building which is quite independent of the DHSS office. Therefore it is important to read carefully the documents telling you where to go and the date of the hearing. It is also important to try and arrive on time. If you are late the tribunal may proceed without you. If you find that you are going to be late it is important to ring a message through; you probably will not have a telephone number for the building where the tribunal is meeting; therefore ring your DHSS office and insist that a message be conveyed immediately to the clerk to the tribunal – preferably indicating how late you are likely to be.

You may find that you have to wait for your hearing. Often the proceedings go behind schedule. When the tribunal members are ready to receive you, the clerk will call you from the waiting room.

What happens at the tribunal

The chairman should explain that the tribunal is independent and wishes to give you a fair hearing. Usually the chairman will ask the spokesman from the DHSS to read out the reasons for the original decision and to mention any relevant facts and law. The chairman will ask you or your representative to explain why you are appealing and why you think your appeal should succeed. The chairman and members may ask both the DHSS representative and you and your representative (and witnesses) questions.

You will be asked to leave when everyone has said all that is necessary; the tribunal clerk will send you the written decision of the tribunal within a few days of the hearing. If you are at a national insurance appeal hearing, the clerk will ask you to leave the room and wait for a while. You will either be called back into the hearing room for the decision of the tribunal, or the clerk will bring it to you. This is only in brief form and full details will be sent on to you a few days later. If the tribunal 'finds against you' you will be given details of how to appeal to the Social Security Commissioner. If you win your appeal, any money due to you (perhaps your benefit has been stopped for a time or perhaps you should have been receiving more) will be backdated to the date of your appeal or the date when benefit was stopped.

Examples of cases taken to appeal

Widows benefit can only be denied on grounds of alleged cohabitation (or re-marriage) and most women who appeal have not been denied benefits completely but have queries about the amount of their benefit.

What is cohabitation?

First of all, there is the situation of the widow denied entitlement to both her widow's pension and supplementary benefit because of the cohabitation rule. The cohabitation rule may seem unjust but it also applies to men claiming supplementary benefit. The problems with administering the rule are such that sometimes widows are accused of cohabiting when in fact they are not. The Widows' Advisory Service has received many letters from widows who have taken in lodgers to supplement their income and subsequently their pension or other benefit has suddenly stopped. It is in this sort of situation that an appeal often becomes necessary.

The following example illustrates the sort of circumstances in which cohabitation may be alleged by the DHSS and where on appeal the widow concerned is found not to be cohabiting.

Mrs Andrews, aged 62, had her four children (all boys) living with her. She was drawing a widowed mother's allowance because the youngest was still at school. One day, without warning, an official of the DHSS called at her home and demanded that she hand him her order book. When she asked why she was told that the DHSS believed she was cohabiting.

The circumstances of the case were that about four years after her husband's death an anonymous letter sent to the DHSS had obviously resulted in her home being watched. The 'Snooper' had seen a man go into her house late at night and leave early in the morning. The man was in fact 25 years younger than her, friendly with her sons, and had worked for the family business that she and her husband had established. She had continued to run the business. The man sometimes slept on the sofa if he was in the area. Occasionally he helped with some of the decorating and gardening. Sometimes he ate meals with the family and watched the family television. The DHSS argued that these circumstances constituted cohabitation.

Mrs Andrews was asked to repay over £5,000 which she had received in benefit since the cohabitation was alleged to have begun.

She went unrepresented to the local tribunal and lost. Two years later her case was heard by the Commissioner, and the Widows' Advisory Service representative was able to get her to explain the situation clearly. The Commissioner decided that she was not cohabiting and she subsequently received over £3,500 in benefit – due to her for the period from when her book was taken away to the date when she was found to be 'not guilty'.

Making a late claim

For most national insurance benefits there are time limits within which you must make your claim. For example, to make a valid claim for widow's allowance you must apply within three months of your husband's death.

However, it is possible to make a late claim if you can show 'good cause' for the delay. Sometimes it is not possible to convince the local DHSS office that you did have good cause for submitting a late claim and you may have to appeal to the local National Insurance Appeal Tribunal. One rather unusual case illustrates this. A widow felt that her husband should have received sickness benefit for nine months prior to his death (he died from cancer).

Mrs Brown's husband had failed to get sickness benefit because his doctor did not believe he was unfit for employment and had therefore refused to issue a sick note. It was not until shortly before he died that cancer was diagnosed. The Widows' Advisory Service suggested that Mrs Brown put in a late claim, on behalf of her husband, for sickness benefit during the relevant period. She had to argue that she could show good cause because circumstances had subsequently shown that had the illness been diagnosed earlier her husband would undoubtedly have been given the medical evidence required to make a successful application for sickness benefit. The tribunal found the argument convincing and paid her the benefit that her husband would have received had the doctor known his condition.

Is bereavement a sickness?

Sickness benefit can be denied to people who the DHSS feels are not sick and to people who it is felt are engaging in activities which are 'prejudicial to recovery'. An example of the former is given below and an example of the latter might be gardening when you are off sick due to a back injury!

A widow had been denied sickness benefit; her sick note from her doctor cited 'bereavement' as her illness. Thus she did not receive either the sickness benefit or the earnings related supplement (this was in the days before the new Statutory Sick Pay scheme came in) to which she would otherwise have been entitled nor would her employer pay her sick benefit!

However, she was advised to approach the DHSS again and since the doctor was actually treating her with tranquilizers she did eventually receive her sickness benefit and earnings related supplement, backdated to the relevant period after the beginning of her incapacity to work. In this case an appeal to the local national insurance tribunal was not necessary: the DHSS 'reviewed their original decision' without seeking confirmation of a tribunal. Had this widow not protested she would have lost over £50 benefit due to her.

(Note that this widow was entitled to sickness benefit because her widow's benefit was not payable at the full rate due to insufficient contributions having been made by her husband.)

Special needs

In practice there are not many appeals about the supplementary benefit weekly scale rates because these are laid down by Parliament; but there can be problems of how to apply the scale rates, as shown by the example below.

Mrs Morris, who suffered from a progressive spinal condition, was experiencing great financial problems. She was in receipt of an age-related widow's pension and a small amount of supplementary benefit. At the time of contacting the Widows' Advisory Service, she was in a distraught state because she did not have the money to pay her electricity bill. The Service helped her out of her immediate difficulty and asked the social services department to negotiate with the DHSS. She applied for an increase in her weekly benefit. Because the DHSS turned down her application, she appealed (with the social worker's help) to the Social Security Appeal Tribunal.

On her behalf the social worker took along detailed calculations of her weekly expenses and a letter from her doctor explaining her need for warm rooms. The tribunal awarded her additional weekly benefit because of her medical condition and the fact that the house was difficult to heat.

Getting help with appeals

The examples given in this chapter have been included to encourage you to think about your own situation. You should always take advice if you are in any doubt as to whether you are receiving all the benefits you are entitled to as a result of insurance contributions and taxes paid by your husband or yourself. There are a lot of sources of advice, including local CABs, local advice centres, social services departments, the Widows' Advisory Service and Cruse branches. We should also end this chapter by saying that the law is not easy for staff at the DHSS and housing departments to understand either!

Making the Most of Yourself

*June Hemer here writes from her personal experience
including fifteen years with the National Association for Widows.*

We have written in earlier chapters about many of the practical things that you can do to make your life as a widow more tolerable and rewarding. We now turn to look at more personal things.

Looking after your appearance

It is often said that women 'dress up only to please men'. I have never subscribed to this view, for there is no greater boost to morale for any woman than to know she looks nice – yes, and even that she smells nice. Yet it is surprising how many times I hear a widow ask, 'What is the use of bothering when there is no-one to see?'. It is true that your husband is no longer around to say 'You look nice', but most of us have sons and daughters and other visitors; and how much more likely are they to continue to visit if they can see that we are caring for ourselves, and our surroundings.

The most important thing, however, is that we feel good ourselves because we have taken the trouble to make ourselves look nice. As we get older, personal hygiene is increasingly important. Frequent baths and changes of clothing are a must to avoid the smell of old age. It need not be an expensive business, water is freely available, and soap and talcum powder are cheap. Hair does not need to be elaborately set, shampoos are inexpensive and what nicer sight is there than white hair that is really white, or brown hair which has a shine? Most hairdressers these days have special days with cheap rates for elderly people and may even have model mornings or evenings when you can get at least a wash and shampoo, and perhaps even a new style, for nothing or a nominal charge. In some areas the Red Cross have personal grooming therapy services, run by volunteers (trained by professionals) for those who are housebound or in hospital to provide hair care, facial massage and manicuring. These services are free but you can make a donation if you want to.

We have already mentioned ways of keeping your wardrobe replenished in the chapter '*Making the Most of Your Money*'. Reputable mail order firms, through which you can get clothes and shoes chosen from a catalogue, allow you to change goods if they do not fit, or even if you don't like them when you see them.

Getting a well-balanced diet

One of the things which distresses most widows is cooking for one – and eating alone. We, perhaps more than most, need nutritious, well-balanced meals. Not only does our health depend on eating well and regularly but so do our looks and moods. Long years of being a widow taught me that if I wanted to retain my independence and not be a burden on my family (and hold down a job!) I had to get into a routine of looking after myself. I know how easy it is to slide into a 'can't be bothered' attitude. It does need self-discipline – but it is well worth the effort involved.

Unfortunately only some shops and supermarkets cater for single people but many have self-service fruit and vegetable counters so that you can buy the quantity you need (you might even be able to get a small bit of cucumber!). But bacon, cheese, meat and so on almost always come in packs far too big. Oh, for the days of the corner shop and the small grocer who was always willing to cut small quantities. Many younger people have no idea how warm and friendly shopping used to be – now it is a cold, hard business, to be got through as quickly as possible.

Many of you have freezers, or freezer compartments in fridges, so that you can buy two chops instead of one, or more meat than you need for one meal. Then you can cook two meals, and freeze one so that you will not have to have the same meal two days running.

Cooking for one can be quite exciting, as the Delia Smith series on television 'One is Fun' showed so well. Even I was amazed at the variety of meals and the speed and ease with which they were prepared – and she caters for all income groups. You can buy her book or borrow it from the library (see page 110).

Why not try out the 'new' healthier foods like yoghurt, beans and lentils and the more unusual fruits and vegetables? Be adventurous, and why not try watching programmes on vegetarian cooking on television for useful ideas?

A joint of meat is probably the food we all miss most. Why not get together with two or three friends and take it in turns to provide Sunday lunch? That way you have the bonus of company as well as the opportunity to cook a proper meal. It need not be restricted to Sunday lunch – company is always lovely.

Sadly it seems to be a favourite concept that we should not treat ourselves to the occasional luxury. Why not? It is worth bothering for yourself. And why not set the table in a way worthy of the meal you have prepared? I still wonder at my spinster aunt who always, at every meal, laid her table immaculately, even to a crisp serviette in a ring. How she would have shuddered at my meals on a small table in front of the television.

Things to be treated with caution

Most of us at sometime try to escape from the reality in which we find ourselves, and it is only too easy to become dependent on alcohol, cigarettes and pills.

In the same way as we have to be careful about our diet, we also have to be careful about drinking alcohol, which can be both expensive and harmful. There's nothing wrong with a social drink – indeed, at a local club or pub it can be a very good thing. But why not agree among your drinking friends not to buy each other rounds, but simply to buy your own when you are thirsty.

Everyone knows that smoking is bad for you. But if you thought it was too late to give up in old age, 'because the damage has already been done', you are wrong. If you continue to smoke you increase your chances of heart disease, cancer and bronchitis; smoking also increases the chances of an infection becoming a serious illness. Older people have a slower rate of recovery from infectious disease, and smoking depletes the body's supply of vitamin C, which helps us to fight infection.

Giving up smoking can be a social activity. You will probably find that in your area there are group meetings organised to help you to stop smoking. It is easier in a group situation because it is awful if you are the only one who has given in to the craving.

It seems almost inevitable that in the first few days after we are widowed we have difficulty in sleeping, and the doctor will have prescribed tranquillisers or sleeping pills, or perhaps both. All too often I hear widows say 'I could not get through the day without my tablets', and 'If I did not have sleeping pills I could never sleep'. Many widows continue to use drugs after the initial shock has worn off and some become addicted to them. The risk of addiction is in fact quite high. We hear much about addiction to hard drugs like heroin and morphine but little about the widespread addiction to sleeping pills and tranquillisers like Librium and Ativan.

Because many widows feel anxious and fearful, and think that there is no-one to understand them and talk to about their grief, they seek relief in drugs and alcohol – hoping to dull the pain of bereavement and inadequacy. Of course, drugs and alcohol do give temporary relief but they are certainly no cure. Once their effect has worn off, the future still has to be faced.

Family doctors are coming to recognise that, rather than repeat prescriptions for sedatives and tranquillisers, widows need repeated reassurance that their grief is normal and that they should talk about their fears. But there is evidence that older people take more drugs than younger people and that they tend to suffer more severely from the side-effects because our metabolism slows up as we grow older – drugs linger in our bodies longer. One in five elderly people take three or more different medicines each day, and one in ten of us takes four or more daily; these are in addition to the over-the-counter drugs like aspirin, paracetamol and cold remedies. About a third of prescriptions for elderly people are repeat prescriptions.

If you find yourself using alcohol or drugs (other than those which you have to take for specific illnesses or conditions) regularly, then you might join a local Widows Advisory Service or a branch of Cruse, where you will be able to share your grief and find alternative forms of support. To help yourself and your doctor monitor the usefulness of your drugs (especially any tranquillisers and sleeping pills), you may want to read Age Concern's book *'Know Your Medicines'* (see page 110).

Finding new interests

Taking care of our minds is at least as important as taking care of our bodies, especially as we get older. Without the stimulus of interesting leisure pursuits, it is all too easy to sink into depression and apathy.

There is, of course, a whole range of activities you can take up, including evening classes for hobbies of all kinds – from cake decoration to car maintenance, pottery to public speaking – and the chance to study seriously for educational qualifications you may often have wished you had the opportunity to acquire earlier. Many people over 60 take Open University courses and even gain degrees – fancy being able to call yourself 'Mary Brown B.A.' at the age of 65!

One of the worst problems may be what to do for your holidays. If you have no special hobby for which holidays are organised (like painting) then you might go on holiday with Saga. Their holidays, both at home and abroad, are designed especially for the elderly, are not unduly expensive and are wonderfully well organised. The International Federation of Widows and Widowers Organisations (the National Association for Widows is a member organisation) can put its members in touch with each other so that exchange holidays can be arranged.

Closer to home is the pleasure an older woman can rediscover in dancing. It is a delightful reason for dressing up. Many dancing schools now have classes for pensioners, and many local voluntary organisations like Age Concern have regular dance groups. You may meet very pleasant men there, but happily it is neither embarrassing nor disapproved of for women to dance together (as it still is for men!).

None of us can be sure what we can do until we try.

Terry Lee found that joining a widow's support group helped her to become a whole person again.

Last year I became a widow and hated that awful word
So many screams inside that only by me were heard.
The children gave much comfort but how could they understand
That I had lost a beloved limb and now lived in an alien land.

But I faced that I was widowed.
I found friends who felt as I did.

They held out their hands and hearts to me
In friendship, love and sympathy.
They were the torch that gave the light so I could see
There was still a life in this world for me.

Thank you my friends with all my heart,
I am not alone. I am a part
Of that band of women who soldier on
When the love of their life in this world has gone.

I am a widow, despite the tears
Despite the problems and the fears
I too said how could I live
Without him beside me, my love to give.

Yet I'm living again and so much is due
To my widowed friends, you, you and you.

Getting Advice and Help

*I*n Part Two of this book we suggest that you contact people in the community who can give you the latest information about things like State benefits and housing. We also refer to other books and to free government leaflets available in pubic libraries, town halls, Citizens Advice Bureaux and at local Widows' Advisory Service centres and branches of Cruse.

Here we give the addresses and phone numbers of many useful organisations, and we list the full titles of many books, pamphlets, and free leaflets. The index will help you find your way to the subjects covered in Part Two.

Useful Organisations

Age Concern
See the description of Age Concern on page 118. Look for the address of your local group in the telephone book. The addresses of the four national centres for local groups are given at the right and below.

Age Concern England
Bernard Sunley House
60 Pitcairn Road,
Mitcham, Surrey,
London CR4 3LL.
Tel: 01 - 640 5431

Age Concern Scotland
33 Castle Street
Edinburgh EH2 3DN.
Tel: 031-225 5000

Age Concern Wales
1 Park Gove, Cardiff
South Glamorgan.
Tel: 0222-371566 or 371821

Age Concern N. Ireland
6 Lower Crescent,
Belfast BT7 1NR.
Tel: 0232-245729

Association of Carers
Advises on services available to carers and offers support.

1st Fl., 21-3 New Rd.,
Chatham,
Kent ME4 4QJ.
Tel: 0634-813981

Child Poverty Action Group
Its local groups help with claims and appeals about welfare rights. Contact the Citizens Rights Office at the Child Poverty Action Group headquarters.

1 Macklin Street,
Drury Lane,
London WC2B 5NH.
Tel: 01 - 405 5942
(Mon. to Fri. 2 - 5.30pm)

Citizens Advice Bureau
Local bureaux provide advice and information on all kinds of problems and will give the name of legal aid solicitors. Also useful for counselling about money problems. The address of the national headquarters is given at the right.

115 - 123 Pentonville Rd.,
London N1 9LZ.
Tel: 01-833 2181

Commission for Local Administration
Commissioners deal with complaints about
local authority administration

**21 Queen Anne's Gate,
London SW1H 9BU.
Tel: 01 - 222 5622**

Community Health Council
Bring complaints and suggestions to the
attention of the District Health Authority.

*Usually listed under
Community in the
telephone directory.*

Consumers Association
Tests, compares and reports on goods and
services in its magazines and books.

**PO Box 44,
Hertford SG14 1SH.
Tel: 0992 59031**

Counsel and Care for the Elderly
A charity which also provides information
on private and voluntary residential
accommodation, nationwide.

**131 Middlesex Street,
London E1 7JF.
Tel: 01 - 621 1624**

**Cruse: The National Organisation for the
Widowed and their Children**
See full description of CRUSE on page 119.
Offers comprehensive service of counselling
by trained people, advice and literature on
practical matters and opportunities for
social contact. Write for your local address.

**Cruse House,
126 Sheen Road,
Richmond, Surrey,
TW9 1UR.
Tel: 01 - 940 4818**

Disability Alliance
Its educational and research departments
run a welfare rights advice service and
produce publications.

**25 Denmark Street,
London WC2 8NJ.
Tel: 01 - 240 0806**

Disabled Living Foundation
Information about aids for disabled people.
Some are on display at their centres in
Birmingham, Caerphilly, Leicester,
Liverpool and Newcastle upon Tyne.

**380/384 Harrow Road,
London W9 2HU.
Tel: 01 - 289 6111**

Family Practitioner Committee
Responsible for the administration of the
services of GPs, dentists, opticians and
chemists. Receives complaints and decides
whether to investigate.

*Usually listed under
Family in the telephone
directory.*

Disablement Income Group
A trust concerned with research, advice and
information for disabled people. Write for
the name of a local branch.

**Attlee House,
28 Commercial Road,
London E1 6LR.
Tel: 01 - 247 2128**

General Medical Council
Oversees standards of medical training and practice. Receives complaints about misconduct by a GP or hospital doctor.

44 Hallam Street,
London W1N 6AE.
Tel: 01 - 580 7642

GRACE
(Mrs Gould's Residential Advisory Centre for the Elderly)
Information on private residential and nursing homes in southern England (not Greater London). A booking fee is charged.

PO Box 71,
Cobham,
Surrey KT11 2JR.
Tel: (093 266) 2928/5765

Health Service Commissioner
Investigates complaints about maladministration and failure to provide proper health services.

for England,
Church House,
Great Smith Street,
London SW1P 3BW.
Tel: 01 - 212 7676

for Wales,
3rd Floor, Queen's Court,
Plymouth Street,
Cardiff CF1 4DA.
Tel: (0222) 394621

Help the Aged
Raises funds for projects around the world. In the UK, funds rehabilitation units, day hospitals, day centres, medical research, minibuses and housing repair schemes. Publishes a monthly newspaper, *YOURS*.

St. James's Walk,
London EC1R 0BE.
Tel: 01 - 253 0253

Housing Corporation
Funds, supervises registered housing associations. Has regional officers.

Maple House,
149 Tottenham Crt. Rd.,
London W1P 0BW.
Tel: 01 - 387 9466

Ladies Assurance Services
A financial advisory service for women by women.

Mrs Andrea Ufland
45 Marloes Road,
London W8 6LA.
Tel: 01 - 937 4119

Law Centres Federation
Supports and advises law centres in the UK. List of local centres available.

Duchess House,
18 - 19 Warren Street,
London W1P 5DB.
Tel: 01 - 387 8570

Law Society
Publishes lists of solicitors who practice
under legal aid scheme.

113 Chancery Lane,
London WC2A 1PL.
Tel: 01 - 242 1222

MIND
(National Association of Mental Health)
Provides information and advice about
mental health. and gives free representation
at mental health review tribunals.

22 Harley Street,
London W1N 2ED.
Tel: 01 - 637 0741

Money Advice Centre
Provides expert advice on all finances,
specialising in debt counselling.

The Birmingham
Settlement,
318 Summerlane,
Birmingham B19.
Tel: 021-359 3562

National Association for Widows
See full description of NAW on page 119.
Seeks to improve the status of widows.
Local groups also provide social activities.

Chell Road,
Stafford ST16 2QA.
Tel: (0785) 58946/45465

**National Council for Carers and their
Elderly Dependants**
Provides advice and information to people
who care for elderly people at home. Has a
network of local groups.

29 Chilworth Mews
London, W2 3RG.
Tel: 01 - 262 1451

National Federation of Consumer Groups
Can put you in touch with your local
consumer group.

12 Mosley Street,
Newcastle upon Tyne,
NE1 1DE.
Tel: 0632 618/259

National Housewives Register
Encourages the formation of discussion
groups on a wide range of subjects.

245 Warwick Road,
Solihull,
Birmingham, B92 7AW.
Tel: 021-706-1101

New Homes Marketing Board
Provides list of builders of housing suitable
for elderly people.

82 New Cavendish St.,
London, W1M 8AD.
Tel: 01-580 5588

**Parliamentary Commissioner and Health
Service Commissioner**
Hear complaints about bad administrative
practices in government departments such
as the DHSS and the Inland Revenue.

Church House,
Great Smith Street,
London, SW1P 3BW.
Tel: 01 - 212 7676

Patients Association
Gives help and advice to individuals and promotes understanding and goodwill between patients and those in medical practice and related fields.

Room 33,
18, Charing Cross Rd.,
London WC2H 0HR.
Tel: 01 - 240 0671

RADAR
(Royal Association for Disability and Rehabilitation)
Provides advice and information on all disabilities and has a comprehensive publications list.

25 Mortimer Street,
London W1N 8AB.
Tel: 01 - 637 5400

Registered Nursing Home Association
Provides information on registered nursing homes throughout the UK.

75 Portland Place,
London W1N 4AN.
Tel: 01 - 631 1524

RELEASE
Advises on legal, criminal and drug related problems. Operates 24hr emergency service.

c/o 347A Upper St.,
London N1
Tel: 01 - 485 4440
　　　01 - 837 5602
　　　01 - 603 8654

SHAC
(Shelter Housing Aid Centre)
Gives advice and help with housing problems to people in London. See its publications listed on page 111.

189A Old Brompton Rd.,
London SW5 0AP.
Tel: 01 - 373 7276

Shelter
A campaigning organisation for the homeless. Also gives advice and assistance with housing problems through a national network of offices. Publishes leaflets and the magazine *ROOF*.

157 Waterloo Rd.,
London SE1 8XN.
Tel: 01 - 633 9377

103 Morrison St.,
Edinburgh.
Tel: 031-229/8771

Widows' Advisory Service
Provides an advice service for widows by widows, including representation at tribunals. Full description on page 119.

Chell Road,
Stafford ST16 2QA.
Tel: (0785) 58946/45465

Useful Leaflets and Books

Free leaflets

These leaflets listed below are available from Citizens Advice Bureaux, central and local offices of the respective government departments or local authorities.

Counsel and Care for the Elderly
Claiming Supplementary Pension Towards Fees for a Registered Private Home

Department of Energy
Make the Most of Your Heating
All About Loft, Tank and Pipe Insulation

Department of the Environment
Controlled Tenancies
Home Improvement Grants
Letting Rooms in Your Home
Letting Your Home or Retirement Home
Mobile Homes
National Mobility Scheme
Notice to Quit
Regulated Tenancies
Service Charges in Flats
Shared Ownership
Tenants Exchange Scheme
The Rent Act and You
Want to Buy Your Home?
Your Home and Compulsory Purchase

Department of Health and Social Security
Attendance Allowance NI.205
Child Benefit CH.1
Child's Special Allowance NI.93
Christmas Bonus NI.229
Death Grant NI.49
Divorced NI.95
Earning Extra Pension by Cancelling Your Retirement NI.92
Fares to Hospital H.11
Going into Hospital NI.9
Help for Handicapped People HB.1
Help with Heating Costs SB.17
How to Appeal NI.246
Industrial Death Benefit NI.10
Industrial Injuries NI.2
Injured at Work FB.15
Invalid Care Allowance NI.212
Invalidity Benefit NI.16A
Living Together as Husband and Wife NI.247
Looking After Someone at Home (Home Responsibilities Protection) NP.27
Mobility Allowance NI.211, NI.243
NHS Dental Treatment D.11
NHS Glasses G.11
NHS Prescription P.11
National Insurance Guide for Widows NI.51
Non-Contributory Invalidity Pension NI.210
Non-Contributory Retirement Pension for People over 80 NI.184
Part-Time Work and Social Security Benefits NI.242
Pensions for Widows of Men Aged 65 or over in July 1948 NI.177A
Rates of War Pensions and Allowances MPL.154
Retirement Benefits for Married Women NP.32B
Retirement Pension NP.32
Retirement Pension for Married Women NP.32B
Retirement Pensions & Widows Benefit:
Payment into Bank or Building Society NI.105
Severe Disablement Allowance NI.252
Social Security Benefit: Rates and Earnings Rules NI.196
Supplementary Benefit leaflets SB.1, SB.8, SB.16, SB.18, SB.19, SB.21

Voluntary Work and Social Security Benefits NI.240
War Widows MPL 152
What to Do After A Death D.49
Which Benefit? 60 Ways to Get Cash Help FB.2
Who Pays Less Rent and Rates? RR.1
Widowed or Divorced Retirement Pension NP.32A
Widowed Mother's Allowance NP.36
Widow's Allowance (first 26 weeks) BW.1 & NP.35
Widow's Pension (after 26 weeks) NP.36
Your Retirement Pension NP.32

Electricity and Gas Boards
Paying Gas and Electricity Bills: How to get Help.

Housing Corporation
Open Door, An Opportunity to Buy a Home of Your Own.

Inland Revenue
Income Tax and Age Allowance IR4A
Income Tax and Capital Gains Tax IR45
Income Tax and Capital Gains Tax Appeals IR37
Income Tax and Pensioners IR4
Income Tax and Widows IR23

Law Society
Legal Aid Guide
Legal Aid — Financial Limits
Small Claims in the County Court

Office of Fair Trading
Dear Shopper in Northern Ireland
Dear Shopper in Scotland
How to cope with Doorstep Salesmen
How to Put Things Right
Leaflets about Codes of Practice (i.e. Buying by Post,
Electrical Goods, etc.)
Stop and Think
There's More to Credit than Just HP

Radar
Housing Grants and Allowances for Disabled People

Solid Fuel Advisory Service
All about Keeping Warm: for those on Pensions or Low Incomes
Heat Your Home Safely

Age Concern Factsheets free on receipt of SAE
Help with Heating **No 1**
Sheltered Housing for Sale **No 2**
Television Licence Concessions **No 3**
Holidays for Elderly People **No 4**
Dental Care in Retirement **No 5**
Companions and Living-in Help **No 6**
Making Your Will **No 7**
Accommodation for Elderly People — Housing Schemes **No 8**
Accommodation in Greater London for Elderly People **No 9**
Local Authorities and Residential Care **No 10**
Supplementary Benefit for Residential Care and Nursing Homes **No 11**
Raising an Income from Your Home **No 12**
Improving and Repairing Your Home — Sources of Financial Help for Elderly Owner-Occupiers **No 13**
Building Society Interest and Income Tax **No 14**
State Pensions: The Earnings Rule and How Pensions are Taxed **No 15**
Supplementary Benefit and Savings/Capital **No 16**
Housing Benefit **No 17**
Carrying on Working after Pension Age and Cancelling Retirement **No 18**
Carrying on Working After Pension Age and Drawing a Retirement Pension **No 19**
National Insurance Contributions and Retirement Pensions up to 1948 **No 20**
National Insurance Contributions and Retirement Pensions 1948-1975 **No21**
National Insurance Contributions and Retirement Pensions 1975 Onwards **No 22**
VAT Relief on the Purchase of Ambulances and Adapted Minibuses **No 23**
Housing Schemes for Elderly People Where a Capital Sum is Required **No 24**
Supplementary Benefit **No 25**

Books to buy or borrow

Here are some books which you may find useful. Ask for them at the library, or you could buy them from a bookshop or the organisation listed.

Age Concern publications

Age Concern England publishes a variety of books for elderly people and those who work with them. Some of these are the publications referred to in the text. Write for a complete catalogue, at the address on page 118

A Buyers' Guide to Sheltered Housing *£1.00*
Better Health in Retirement *£1.20*
Gardening in Retirement *£1.95*
Heating Help in Retirement *£1.00*
Know Your Medicines *£3.75*
Staying Put: Help for Older Home Owners *£0.55*
Your Housing in Retirement *£1.20*
Your Taxes and Savings in Retirement *£1.70*
Your Rights for Pensioners *£0.90*
Prices include postage and packing

Other publications

All in the End is Harvest; An anthology for those who grieve, by Agnes Whitaker, Darton, Longman and Todd, 1984, *£3.95*
Before I Go, by Mary Stott, Virago, 1985, *£4.50*
Bereavement: Studies of Grief in Adult Life, by Colin Murray Parks, Penguin, 1975, *£2.50*
Fair Deal, published by Office of Fair Trading, available from HMSO bookshops *£0.95*
Handywoman by Sonia Mills, Corgi Books 1985. *£3.95*
How it Feels When a Parent Dies, by Jill Kremner, Gollancz 1983. *£5.95*
On Your Own, by Jean Shapiro, Pandora, 1985. *£6.95*
One is Fun, by Delia Smith, Hodder and Stoughton, 1985. *£7.95*
Patients' Rights: A Guide for NHS Patients and Doctors, published by National Consumer Council, 1983 *£1.50*
Safety in Retirement, published by ROSPA, Home Safety Division, Canon House, Priory Queensway, Birmingham B4 6BS, *£0.60 inc p&p*
Women and Tranquillisers, by Celia Haddon, Sheldon Press, 1984, *£3.95*

CPAG publications
See page 100 *for address*
National Welfare Benefits Handbook, 1986, *£4.00*
Rights Guide for Non-Means Tested Social Security Benefits,
1986 *£4.00*

SHAC publications
See page 104 *for address*
Buying a Home *£1.00*
Homeless? Know Your Rights *£0.40*
Home Owners: Your Guide to Housing Benefits *£0.60*
Housing Rights Guide *£4.50*
Moving Home in Retirement *£0.85*
Private Tenants: Protection from Eviction *£0.60*
Rights Guide for Home Owners *£2.50*
The Right Move: A Guide to Mobility and Housing *£0.50*
Your Rights to Repairs as a Council Tenant *£1.00*
Your Rights to Repairs as a Private or Housing Association
Tenant *£1.00*

Other Publications from Age Concern England

AGE and VITALITY

Commonsense ways of adding life to years and a detailed look at the positive side of growing older. Includes practical suggestions on how to maintain physical and mental vigour. **£1.30**

BETTER HEALTH IN RETIREMENT

A publication of great assistance in helping people to adapt to retirement and to think positively about their health. A practical approach to keeping fit and an informative guide on health in later life. **£1.20.**

HEATING HELP IN RETIREMENT

Discusses every type of fuel and how to lower costs by choosing the most efficient form of heating. Also deals with draught-proofing, insulation and what to do about fuel debts. An invaluable book for the cost conscious pensioner. **£.100**

GARDENING IN RETIREMENT

Getting the maximum pleasure from gardening with the minimum of effort, expense or even space is the idea behind this book. Written in down to earth terms and with step-by-step drawings and full colour plates. Introduction by Percy Thrower. **£1.95**

Any of these publications can be obtained post free from the address below. Please make cheques/P.O.'s payable to Age Concern England.

Age Concern England
60, Pitcairn Road, Mitcham, Surrey CR4 3LL.

INDEX

About the Book's Sponsors

Four national organisations worked together to produce this book. Royal Life Insurance provided funds; Cruse and the National Association for Widows were responsible for the writing; and Age Concern England for editing, production and publishing.

Royal Life is a major life assurance company providing a wide range of products in the financial services sector. As part of the Royal Insurance Group, one of the largest composite insurance companies in the world, it has enjoyed a tradition of successful management of investment funds dating back to 1803.

As a financially innovative and caring company, it is well aware of the problems faced by many widows who find the constant increases in the costs for heating, housing, food and light such a burden. This is reflected in its continuing support of urban improvement schemes and of the worthwhile work carried out by voluntary organisations.

Address: P.O. Box 30, New Hall Place, Liverpool, L69 3HS.

Age Concern is a network of over 1300 independent local UK groups serving the needs of elderly people, assisted by well over 124,000 volunteers. The wide range of services provided includes day care, visiting services, clubs and specialist services for physically and mentally frail elderly people.

The four national centres, Age Concern England, Scotland, Wales and Northern Ireland give advice and support to their local groups, to professionals and volunteers working with elderly people. The addresses of these centres are given on page 100.

Age Concern England, whose membership includes 70 national organisations, provides research, training and information, as well as publishing a wide range of books. It is a registered charity dependent on public support for the continuation of its work.

Address: Bernard Sunley House, 60 Pitcairn Road, Mitcham, Surrey CR4 3LL.

Cruse, the National Organisation for the Widowed and their Children, is a registered charity with over 100 branches in Britain. It offers help through counselling for the individual and in groups; it provides advice and information on practical problems and opportunities for social contact. Cruse runs training courses for health care professionals and its own volunteer counsellors and conducts research into aspects of bereavement. Special publications include the monthly *Cruse Chronicle* for members, a wide range of factsheets and leaflets, and *Bereavement Care*, a journal for all who help the bereaved.

Address: Cruse House, 126 Sheen Road, Richmond, Surrey TW9 1UR.

The National Association for Widows (NAW) was founded in 1971 as a pressure group seeking an improved tax position and better pensions for widows. It has over 3000 members, and where there are local branches, these provide the basis of social activities and support for local Widows' Advisory Services.

In 1974 the Association set up a Trust to administer the Widows' Advisory Service; in 1975 the Trust was awarded charitable status. Local advisory services are provided by volunteers. Support for the local groups, and for individual widows who either do not live near a local service or have a very complex problem is given from the national headquarters in Stafford. The Association produces a regular *Newsletter,* and the Trust publishes useful leaflets such as *Home Help for Widows.*

Address: Chell Road, Stafford ST16 2QA.